Mothers of the Church

of the

The Witness of Early Christian Women

Mike Aquilina and Christopher Bailey

Our Sunday Visitor Publishing Division
Our Sunday Visitor, Inc.
Huntington, Indiana 46750

Copyright © 2012 by Mike Aquilina and Christopher Bailey. Published 2012.

17 16 15 14 13 12   1 2 3 4 5 6 7 8 9

ISBN: 978-1-61278-562-2 (Inventory No. T1260)
eISBN: 978-1-61278-210-2
LCCN: 2011944060

Cover design: Amanda Falk
Cover image: Basilica of Sant'Apollinare Nuovo in Ravenna, Italy: "Procession of the Holy Virgins and Martyrs"
Interior design: M. Urgo

PRINTED IN THE UNITED STATES OF AMERICA

Mothers
of the
Church

For Teresa and Terri

Table of Contents

Acknowledgments

In spite of the names on the cover, the real originator of this book and its title is Teresa Bailey. It was she who said to her husband: "Why haven't you and Mike written a book about the Mothers of the Church? I mean, everyone knows about the Fathers of the Church, but what about the Mothers?"

Its other progenitor, of course, is Terri Aquilina. These are two women who have spent their lives modeling the strength of character and intellect that made the women in these pages so memorable. They are mothers, writers, thinkers, leaders, and — since they have to live with us — martyrs.

In producing the book itself, we had the enormous advantage of living in the digital age. Primary sources that would have taken us years to track down before the Internet came along are now easily searchable on line. But they're available only because of the heroic volunteers who digitized these sources in the first place. Among those volunteers, we must especially express our gratitude to Roger Pearse (Tertullian.org), whose work has made many of the rarest texts of early Christianity accessible to everyone, and to Kevin Knight (NewAdvent.org), who keeps a digital library of the standard editions of the Church Fathers so that everyone can apply all the power of a modern search engine to them. Many other online collectors have helped us with obscure sources, and we're grateful to all of them.

As the work on this book came to a close, Teresa told us: "I can't believe *I* had to think of that for you." But it doesn't seem unbelievable to the authors at all.

Abbreviations

We've tried to keep confusing abbreviations to a minimum, but the standard editions of the early Christian writers in English are two series with unwieldy titles. We've abbreviated them this way:

- **ANF**: *The Ante-Nicene Fathers: Translations of the Writings of the Fathers Down to A.D. 325.* Edited by the Rev. Alexander Roberts, D.D., and James Donaldson, LL.D. (New York: Charles Scribner's Sons, 1903).

- **NPNF1**: *A Select Library of the Nicene and Post-Nicene Fathers of the Christian Church.* Edited by Philip Schaff, D.D., LL.D. (New York: The Christian Literature Company, 1887).

- **NPNF2**: *A Select Library of the Nicene and Post-Nicene Fathers of the Christian Church, Second Series.* Edited by Philip Schaff, D.D., LL.D., and Henry Wace, D.D. (New York: The Christian Literature Company, 1890).

The abbreviations are followed by the volume and page number so that, for example, "*NPNF2* 10:364" means that the passage is found in the *Nicene and Post-Nicene Fathers, Second Series*, volume 10, page 364.

Many of the quotations from the Mothers and Fathers of the Church are taken from the versions of these texts hosted at New Advent (NewAdvent.org) and the Tertullian Project (Tertullian.org), with the kind permission of the compilers of those sites, Kevin Knight and Roger

Pearse, respectively. We have updated the language of some of the older translations, to make them intelligible to modern readers.

Chapter 1

The Christian Revolution

"There is neither Jew nor Greek, there is neither slave nor free, there is neither male nor female; for you are all one in Christ Jesus" (Galatians 3:28).

When St. Paul wrote those famous words, he was lobbing a verbal grenade at the established order of things. And he knew it.

It was possible for a Greek in the Roman Empire to imagine that Jews were human too. Although they had different customs, they did have a long intellectual tradition, and the more moderate ones could adapt to Greek customs so well that they hardly looked any different from regular people.

And it was just barely possible to imagine that there was no real distinction in nature between slave and free.

After all, slaves might have been princes captured in battle. Only fortune, that notoriously fickle principle, had brought them low, and fortune might do the same to any person one day.

But any reasonable man would draw the line at "neither male nor female." The difference between male and female was the order of nature. Males were superior (a man would say) because women were inferior. It was obvious — so obvious that it hardly needed an argument. Fire is hot, water is wet, and women are inferior to men. This unquestioned and unquestionable truth was the basis of all human society. If Christianity merely denied the old pagan gods, that could have been forgiven — hardly anyone in the better classes really believed in them anyway. But Christianity was a frontal assault on Roman family values, and that made it a danger to the state.

To understand just how dangerous Christianity was, though, we need to have some understanding of Roman family values, and what they meant if you happened to be female.

What Good Was a Girl?

It wasn't easy growing up a girl in the pagan Roman Empire. In fact, there was a good chance a girl wouldn't grow up at all.

Children had no "rights": they belonged to their father, and in theory he had the power of life and death over them. Of course, a boy was valuable, which tended to mitigate the arbitrariness of his father. It would be worth all the trouble and expense to raise a boy to adulthood because he would carry on the family, and he would be there to take care of his parents in their old age.

But what good was a girl? If the parents were lucky, their daughter might marry into a powerful family and make a useful alliance for them. More likely, though, they would have to feed and care for her for fifteen years or so, and then they would have to pay some useless wastrel a ruinous dowry for taking her off their hands. No wonder one of the favorite adjectives for "daughters" was "odious."

There was an alternative, of course. If the child came out a girl, the parents could kill it and spare themselves all that trouble. The mother might have some irrational sentimental attachment to the baby, but since the father owned his wife as well, she had little say in the matter.

If the parents were a bit squeamish about killing a baby outright, they could resort to "exposition" — that is, instead of killing the child, they could just leave it somewhere, usually somewhere off the beaten track. The practical effect was the same — they were rid of an unwanted burden — but if the child died, it was the will of the gods, not their own doing. After all, if the gods really wanted the child to live, they could send a she-wolf to take care of it.

Every once in a while, some construction project or archaeological dig exposes a pile of Roman-era infant skeletons, and the news makes medium-sized headlines around the world. But historians are never surprised. They know that it's just another human garbage dump. The babies were rubbish, thrown away because they were useless to their fathers. Most of them were girls.

It did sometimes happen that someone rescued one of those exposed infants. A Christian who came along and found an abandoned baby would probably pick it up and make sure it was cared for; Christians were irrationally sentimental that way. On the other hand, a slave trader might come along and pick it up as a potentially valuable property. In the early days, when there were more slave traders than Christians, a girl — or for that matter, a boy — rescued from the rubbish heap was most likely to end up in a brothel. That was where someone could easily make money from a child who was too young for useful work. There were brothels that specialized in young children. Brothels were most likely tolerated the way pornography is tolerated today: it might not be everyone's favorite thing, but it's part of the social landscape, and what are you going to do about it? In a society where children really had no "rights," and slaves were property to be disposed of at will, it probably didn't make much sense to worry about what happened to slave children in brothels. If there was a worry, it was only about the moral effect on the patrons.

Between Beast and Barbarian

Rome took her learning, her culture, and her assumptions about the world from Greece. Greek was the everyday language of the eastern half of the empire, but it was also the language of learning throughout. Roman scholars wrote their learned treatises in Greek, just as, centuries later, Renaissance scholars would write theirs in Latin. All the popular schools of philosophy had been founded by Greek thinkers, and Greek learning shaped the attitude of every thinking Roman on just about every subject.

In general, those Greek philosophers had little use for women as people:

> But Hermippus, in his *Lives,* tells about Thales, the story that some tell of Socrates. He used to say that he thanked Fortune for three things. "First, that I was born a human and not a beast. Second, that I was born a man and not a woman. Third, that I was born a Greek and not a barbarian."
>
> — Diogenes Laertius, *Lives of the Philosophers*, 1.33

Halfway between beast and barbarian on the scale of things you don't want to be: that's where a Greek philosopher puts a woman. The best a woman could do was to stay out of the way and be ornamental, as we learn from another famous philosopher:

> He [Antisthenes] said that the wise man would conduct himself, not according to the established laws, but according to the law of virtue. He would marry in order to beget children, choosing the most beautiful woman as his wife. And he would love her: for only the wise man knows what is worth loving.
>
> — Diogenes Laertius, *Lives of the Philosophers*, 6.11

We notice that the *wise* man chooses a woman for her beauty, not for her virtue or her wisdom. Beauty is the thing he loves in her, the thing that makes her worth loving. But what does beauty mean to a wise man? Here's an opinion from that same Antisthenes:

To a young man posing ostentatiously for a sculptor, he [Antisthenes] said, "Tell me, if the bronze could speak, what would it pride itself on?"

He replied, "On its beauty."

"Then are you not ashamed," he said, "to delight in the same thing as an inanimate object?"

— Diogenes Laertius, *Lives of the Philosophers*, 6.9

So the virtue of a woman is the same as the virtue of an inanimate chunk of bronze, and the wise man would be ashamed to admit it as his own virtue.

What we learn from these pagan philosophers is that women were perpetual children. And in that way they were worse off than male children. It's true that children were nobody — they were property — but sons would grow up some day. Even a male slave could hope to buy his freedom eventually if he was thrifty enough. But a woman would always be a woman.

Conditions didn't improve much for women over the centuries between Antisthenes and the height of the Roman Empire. A woman was still not much of a person in the legal sense. As St. Ambrose will point out in his life of St. Agnes, a woman's testimony was not admissible in a court of law. It is certainly true that Roman women could be stubbornly independent, and they probably had more privileges than their Greek counterparts. But for Romans as for Greeks, the general assumption was that a woman was perpetually a child.

The daughters who did grow up didn't have a long childhood. Twelve was considered a marriageable age for a girl, and as soon as she reached that age, her father would start looking for someone to take her off his hands. She had little choice in the matter. Technically, Roman law required that she consent to a marriage. But, technically, Roman law also required her to obey her father if he ordered her to consent, which made the "consent" rather hollow.

Easy Prey

So this was what it was to be a young woman in Rome: you could expect to pass from the control of your father to the control of your husband, and your father would decide who that husband would be. But what about after that?

As a mother, a woman might have some authority over her children. But in families that owned slaves, a nurse was usually assigned to the daily work of childcare, and many pagan writers remember their nurses far more fondly than their mothers. Sons would have another influence as soon as they were old enough to be educated. If the family had any money at all, an educated slave would be assigned as a "tutor" — a teacher who was always with the boys, and in fact would become their chief adult contact. Children were expected to honor their parents, but more in the way they honored the Roman state than out of personal love for them. They might not even know their parents very well.

As a wife, then, a woman might have some status, but it was all contingent on her husband. If he divorced her — and divorce was easy in imperial times — he could leave her destitute, unless there was some kind of prenuptial agreement that she would keep some of her own family property.

Divorce wasn't the only disaster that could happen to a wife. Men often died before their wives. And a widow's life could be very difficult.

St. John Chrysostom's father died shortly after John was born, leaving his mother, Anthusa, a young widow with a baby to take care of. Fortunately, she had money to work with: as a male child, no matter how tiny, young John would have been his father's heir, keeping the inheritance in the immediate family. Still, it was a hard life, and not least because she was surrounded by scheming relatives. Apparently, the way Anthusa describes it, a widow was an easy target for unscrupulous members of her own family: she seems to accept it as simply normal that relatives will try to rip off a widow any way they can. Then there are the tax collectors, and the servants — everyone who has any business dealings with the widow sees her as an easy mark:

> My child, I wasn't allowed to enjoy your father's virtue very long — that was what seemed appropriate to God. He died just after my labor, which made you an orphan, but me a widow before my time, and left me with all the suffering of widowhood. And only those who have gone through it can really know what that's like. No words could express the storm and tempest a girl goes through then. She's just left her father's house, and she has no experience in business — but she's suddenly hit with intolerable grief, and she has to take on a burden more than her youth and her sex can bear. It's necessary, I think, for her to deal with the servants' laziness,

and to protect herself against the traps relatives set for her, and to guard against their dishonesty, and to bear up bravely under the injuries of the tax collectors and the inhuman way they go about their collecting.

If the one who has died has left a child — well, if the child is a girl, even that will cause the mother a lot of care, but not so much worry and fear. But a son fills every one of her days with hope and fear, and with more cares than a daughter does. And I won't even talk about the money she has to spend if she wants to give him a liberal education.

— *NPNF1* 9:34

With no man to protect her, a widow had to be awfully clever just to survive. Some of them were clever and strong: we get the idea from John Chrysostom that Anthusa had a lot of the qualities — dogged tenacity, a keen eye for human motivations, and a natural management sense — that would later make her son such an effective and inspiring bishop. But an ordinary woman — someone who had no more than the average allotment of talent and persistence that most ordinary people have — would be lost in the jungle, even if she had money. If she had no son and no money, her case was worse than hopeless.

Now we begin to see why widows were always at the top of the list of people good Christians had to look out for. No one else was doing it. If even a widow with money was easy prey for schemers and bullies, the ordinary widow must have thought she would be better off dead. Her only hope was to marry someone else as quickly as she could: even if her new husband was a schemer and a bully himself, it was better to have a home than to be begging in the street. But, of course, a widow had to have either money or exceptional good looks to attract a new husband.

A Radical Truth

We've seen now what Roman family values were like: the patriarch of the family was supreme, with theoretical power of life and death over his children, and women were defined not as people but as extensions of the male.

This is where the Christians attacked the fundamental basis of Roman society. Christians spoke directly to "stupid women, little children, and fools," as the pagan philosopher Celsus puts it. He compares Christians to the tricksters in the market who don't dare try to fool an intelligent man but play their tricks on the young and stupid:

> What is said by a few who are considered as Christians, concerning the doctrine of Jesus and the precepts of Christianity, is not designed for the wiser but for the more unlearned and ignorant part of mankind. For this is what they teach: "Let no one who is educated join us, no one who is wise, no one who is prudent (for we think these things are evil); but let anyone who is unlearned, who is stupid, who is an infant in understanding, boldly come to us." For the Christians openly acknowledge that such as these are worthy to be noticed by their God. Thus they show that the only people they want to persuade, and the only ones they *can* persuade, are the ignoble, the senseless, slaves, stupid women, little children, and fools.

When we're in the market, we sometimes see infamous characters and jugglers gathered together, who don't dare show their tricks to intelligent men; but when they perceive a lad, and a crowd of slaves and stupid men, they endeavor to ingratiate themselves with such characters as these.

In just the same way, we see [Christians] in their own houses, wool weavers, shoemakers, fullers, and the most illiterate hicks, who wouldn't dare say anything in the presence of older and wiser fathers of families; but when they meet with children apart from their parents, and certain stupid women with them, then they discuss something amazing: they say, "It isn't proper to pay attention to parents and tutors, but you should be persuaded by us. Your parents and tutors are delirious and stupid: they don't know what is truly good, and they can't make it happen."

— *ANF* 4:486

Christians, says Celsus, are a bunch of illiterate hicks who bypass the fathers and husbands and speak directly to women and children as though they were, well, people. That's exactly what makes Christianity an assault on Roman family values: the Christians assume that women (and children) might have minds, with thoughts in them apart from the thoughts the men who control them have put there.

And Celsus was absolutely right. Christianity *was* a frontal assault on Roman family values. The Christians *did* treat women, and even children, as if they were people with minds of their own. A few pagan philosophers had dabbled with the idea that women had minds equal to men's; they were dismissed as cranks, and their ideas survive only in the incredulous and sneering reports of their contemporaries. Paul said that "there is neither male nor female," and the Christians accepted his dictum as revealed Scripture.

That doesn't mean there is no difference between women and men. There are obvious physical differences, and those exist for a reason. There are also differences in role: try as he might, a man can never bear a child. Men are fathers and women mothers, and those roles are not interchangeable. The Church ordains men and not women; women serve in other roles. But a man is not *superior*: he is not more of a person than a woman, and certainly not more valuable to God.

Many Christians have been far from perfect in the way women have been treated. Most of us have trouble living up to our most radical ideas; we find it much too easy to sink back down into our comfortable prejudices. But the radical truth of Christianity is this: In Christ, there is neither male nor female. Imperfect though they were, the early Christians lived this truth in a way that shocked and perplexed their pagan neighbors.

After more than a millennium and a half, a lot of the documentary evidence of what was going on in women's lives — or men's lives, for that matter — has disappeared. But even what's left is extraordinarily rich. We have stories of all sorts, with wonderful personalities to meet and extraordinary ideas to think about.

Some of these readings are writings by great Christian women. Some of them are recollections of their sayings by the people they taught — which was a very common way of preserving the thoughts of great teachers. (We would have nothing of the words of Socrates or Aristotle or Jesus Christ if their disciples hadn't written down what they said.) And some of these are stories of great Christian women written down by men who admired them — which is perhaps the most remarkable group of writings.

The variety of the women here is striking. We have consecrated virgins, heroic martyrs, and poor widows, but also worldly businesswomen, rich ladies from the upper crust of society, and an indomitable adventurer on a world tour. There are old women at the end of their lives, as well as children who gave up their lives for a greater life in Christ. Once again, in itself the variety teaches us something about the Christian difference. Christian women didn't have one set role in life: they were individuals, and the men around them had to learn to accept them that way.

Mothers of Us All

Which brings us to one final question that someone will almost certainly ask: Why are two men writing a book about the great women of early Christianity?

Well, one reason is that we could hardly help ourselves. When you've heard a great story, the first thing you want to do is pass it on. There are great stories here, and we hope you'll enjoy them as much as we do.

But these women are also our teachers — teachers for the whole Christian Church, not just for Christian women. It would be wrong to consign them to some women's-studies ghetto, as if they were pretty good for girls but not ready for the boys' league yet. These women have something to say to everyone, not just to women, and we owe it to them to take them at least as seriously as their Christian contemporaries took them.

The fact is that these women — who legally couldn't have been witnesses in a court of law — are our witnesses in the court of history and tradition. As the *Catechism of the Catholic Church* points out (n. 688), that is one of the functions of the Church *Fathers*. But it's no less true of the Mothers of the Church. Sts. Monica, Macrina, and Perpetua give us our most vivid witness of the doctrine of purgatory. Monica shows us that votive Masses for the dead were an established fact of Christian practice. And all of the holy virgins of the early years of the Church testify to the high value Christians placed on consecrated virginity (see 1 Corinthians 7).

Chapter 2

Holy Women of the New Testament

Jesus of Nazareth specialized in shocking the sensibilities of the religious establishment of his day. It was easy to do, because the establishment was easily shocked. Heal a blind man on the Sabbath, and you've turned the world upside down.

But there was hardly anything more shocking than the way he treated women. As we see in the story of the Samaritan woman at the well, it even shocked his own followers, who were used to being shocked by their Teacher. "Just then his disciples came. They marveled that he was talking with a woman, but none said, 'What do you wish?' or, 'Why are you talking with her?' " (John 4:27). They "marveled," but by this time they knew better than to second-guess the Teacher. If he wanted to go around talking to Samaritan women, he must have had a good reason. But you can imagine them whispering to one another later that day.

Mary, the Mother of Jesus

The Gospel story is filled with remarkable women. It's hard to think of another ancient writing that has so many strong female characters. Think of how St. Luke tells the story: the main character in the beginning is Mary, the mother of Jesus. In fact, we hear the story of Jesus' birth and childhood mostly from her point of view.

Tradition tells us that's because St. Luke got the story from Mary herself during the time he spent with her and the apostles. And Luke himself gives us broad hints that he heard the story from Mary: "But Mary kept all these things, pondering them in her heart," he tells us (Luke 2:19), after the shepherds visit and tell her about their vision of the angels. And again we read that "his mother kept all these things in her heart" (Luke 2:51), after the story of twelve-year-old Jesus staying behind in the Temple in Jerusalem. If Mary kept these things in her heart, the only way Luke would have heard them is if she had told him. Perhaps Luke, a careful historian, added these little asides to explain why these events appear in his story but not in the other versions of the story that "many have undertaken to compile" (Luke 1:1).

So what kind of woman was this Mary? Well, as Luke tells us, she was nobody considerable from the world's point of view. She lived in Nazareth, a backward little town in Galilee. People of that time could probably tell it right away from her accent. (During the trial of Jesus, Peter was instantly recognized as a Galilean by the way he talked: "Certainly you are also one of them, for your accent betrays you," as one of the crowd says in Matthew 26:73.) Nazareth was not just backward: it was *proverbially* backward. "Can anything good come out of Nazareth?" was Nathanael's first reaction (John 1:46) when Philip told him that Jesus of Nazareth was the Messiah.

But God chose *this* woman: not a refined lady from a royal house in Jerusalem, but a poor young girl from a town in the sticks. This was something scandalous to pagan philosophers. There are natural degrees of perfection in people, the pagan philosophers believed, and in general someone who comes from a good family and has an exalted station in life is obviously more perfect than someone who comes from a town in Galilee. Celsus, one of the most prominent anti-Christian writers of the early Christian era, points out how absurd it is that the Son of God should be born to a poor woman:

> So was the mother of Jesus beautiful, and was God connected with her because of her beauty — even though he is not adapted to be in love with a corruptible body? Isn't it absurd to suppose that God would fall in love with a woman who was neither fortunate nor from a royal family, hardly even known to her neighbors?
>
> — *ANF* 4:413

We might call this the argument from snobbery: surely God would choose someone from the better elements of society, not some lower-class nobody who had to work with her own hands.

But God did choose a poor woman, because God sees through the worldly circumstances to the beauty of the soul. And this is what happened:

In the sixth month the angel Gabriel was sent from God to a city of Galilee named Nazareth, to a virgin betrothed to a man whose name was Joseph, of the house of David; and the virgin's name was Mary. And he came to her and said, "Hail, full of grace, the Lord is with you!" But she was greatly troubled at the saying, and considered in her mind what sort of greeting this might be. And the angel said to her, "Do not be afraid, Mary, for you have found favor with God. And behold, you will conceive in your womb and bear a son, and you shall call his name Jesus.

He will be great, and will be called the Son of the Most
    High;
and the Lord God will give to him the throne of his
    father David,
and he will reign over the house of Jacob for ever;
and of his kingdom there will be no end."
And Mary said to the angel, "How can this be, since I
    have no husband?" And the angel said to her,
"The Holy Spirit will come upon you,
and the power of the Most High will overshadow you;
therefore the child to be born will be called holy,
the Son of God.

And behold, your kinswoman Elizabeth in her old age has also conceived a son; and this is the sixth month with her who was called barren. For with God nothing will be impossible." And Mary said, "Behold, I am the handmaid of the Lord; let it be to me according to your word." And the angel departed from her.

— Luke 1:26-38

We hear that story every year at Christmas, and we're probably a bit deadened to it by now. But try to look at it with new eyes. Notice, first of all, how Luke tells it from Mary's point of view. He even tells us what she was thinking: "But she was greatly troubled at the saying, and considered in her mind what sort of greeting this might be." That's actually quite rare in the Gospels, and it's another sign that Luke heard the story directly from Mary. We're used to novels in which the narrator magically knows all the thoughts in every character's head, but that was not a normal way of writing history in Luke's time. If he tells us what Mary was thinking, it's probably because Mary told him she was thinking it.

But this insight into Mary's private thoughts has another effect. As a narrative technique, it draws us, the hearers of the story, into Mary's point of view. We see the Annunciation with Mary's eyes, and we understand why it's a frightening and baffling experience. Why is this angel suddenly appearing? Have I done something terribly wrong?

It's a scary thing when an angel shows up; usually the first thing the angel has to say is "Do not be afraid."

Mary asks questions too. "How can this be, since I have no husband?"

But when the angel has explained what will happen, Mary has the faith to believe that "with God nothing will be impossible." "Behold, I am the handmaid of the Lord; let it be to me according to your word."

We know that Mary continued to be an important presence in Jesus' life right to the Ascension. She was the occasion of his first miracle, the changing of water into wine at the marriage feast in Cana. We usually read the story for what it tells us about Christ, but let's read it right now for what it tells us about Mary:

> On the third day there was a marriage at Cana in Galilee, and the mother of Jesus was there; Jesus also was invited to the marriage, with his disciples.
>
> When the wine failed, the mother of Jesus said to him, "They have no wine."
>
> And Jesus said to her, "O woman, what have you to do with me? My hour has not yet come."
>
> His mother said to the servants, "Do whatever he tells you."
>
> Now six stone jars were standing there, for the Jewish rites of purification, each holding twenty or thirty gallons. Jesus said to them, "Fill the jars with water." And they filled them up to the brim. He said to them, "Now draw some out, and take it to the steward of the feast." So they took it.
>
> When the steward of the feast tasted the water now become wine, and did not know where it came from (though the servants who had drawn the water knew), the steward of the feast called the bridegroom and said to him, "Every man serves the good wine first; and

when men have drunk freely, then the poor wine; but you have kept the good wine until now."

This, the first of his signs, Jesus did at Cana in Galilee, and manifested his glory; and his disciples believed in him.

— John 2:1-11

"Do whatever he tells you" is a good summary of Mary's message to us. But you'll notice it's not a passive submission; it's an active faith. Mary sees the problem and has the faith to believe that Jesus can solve it. In fact, she's the only one at the party who's ready to take charge. She rounds up the servants and arranges for them to play their parts in the proceedings. Christ is the one who performs the miracle, but Mary is the one who gets everyone in their places and persuades them that a miracle can be performed. She's the prototype of all those strong Christian women who have made the Church work over the centuries — constantly getting things done, putting things in place, and reminding everyone around them, "Do whatever he tells you."

Mary was at the foot of the cross, though it would have been so much easier for her to retire to some private room and say she couldn't stand to watch the crucifixion of her only Son. There, at the cross, Jesus placed her in the care of John, his best friend among the disciples — or placed John in the care of Mary (see John 19:25-27). The last mention of her specifically by name in the Bible is when we see her praying in the upper room with the disciples before Pentecost (see Acts 1:14). But tradition says she spent a long time after that, living with her adopted son John and — among other things — telling Luke the story of her life.

That's where her life on earth ends. But right at the end of our Christian Scriptures, the Revelation to John gives us a powerfully symbolic glimpse of her life in heaven:

> And a great sign appeared in heaven, a woman clothed with the sun, with the moon under her feet, and on her head a crown of twelve stars; she was with child and she cried out in her pangs of birth, in anguish for delivery. And another sign appeared in heaven; behold, a great red dragon, with seven heads and ten horns, and seven diadems upon his heads. His tail swept down a third of the stars of heaven, and cast them to the earth. And the dragon stood before the woman who was about to bear a child, that he might devour her child when she brought it forth; she brought forth a male child, one who is to rule all the nations with a rod of iron, but her child was caught up to God and to his throne, and the woman fled into the wilderness, where she has a place prepared by God, in which to be nourished for one thousand two hundred and sixty days.
>
> — Revelation 12:1-6

The "woman clothed with the sun" gives birth to the Messiah in spite of the dragon, who is Satan. The symbolic imagery of Revelation is deliberately hard to understand; its purpose is to convey a message of hope to Christians and conceal it from the unbelievers. But the picture of Mary crowned with twelve stars seems to make her the representative of God's people — Israel with its twelve tribes and the Christian Church with its twelve apostles.

The Women Who Bankrolled the Ministry

Throughout the ministry of Jesus, women came to him as if he were the only man alive who would listen to their troubles. And Jesus not only listened to them but insisted on making the men around him listen to them as well.

The sinful woman who washed Jesus' feet in the house of Simon the Pharisee (see Luke 7:37-50) gave Jesus the opportunity to teach the Pharisees something about God's forgiveness. The woman who had been bleeding for years declared "in the presence of all the people" that Jesus had healed her (Luke 8:43-48). Mary and Martha brought Jesus into their house, and Jesus actually praised Mary for trying to learn from his teaching instead of doing what her sister thought was proper women's work:

> Now as they went on their way, he entered a village; and a woman named Martha received him into her house. And she had a sister called Mary, who sat at the Lord's feet and listened to his teaching.
>
> But Martha was distracted with much serving; and she went to him and said, "Lord, do you not care that my sister has left me to serve alone? Tell her then to help me."
>
> But the Lord answered her, "Martha, Martha, you are anxious and troubled about many things; one thing is needful. Mary has chosen the good portion, which shall not be taken away from her."
>
> — Luke 10:38-42

The idea that a woman's mind was more important than the menial work she could do must have been terribly shocking, but St. Luke dutifully records the teaching.

Jesus attracted women as followers throughout his ministry, and it's pretty obvious why: other teachers told them to go away, but Jesus talked to women, thus extending to them the same basic human dignity that men enjoyed. We even hear from Luke that some of Jesus' ministry was financed by well-to-do women who had started to follow him:

> Soon afterward he went on through cities and villages, preaching and bringing the good news of the kingdom of God. And the Twelve were with him, and also some women who had been healed of evil spirits and infirmities: Mary, called Magdalene, from whom seven demons had gone out, and Joanna, the wife of Chuza, Herod's steward, and Susanna, and many others, who provided for them out of their means.
>
> — Luke 8:1-3

This is the first mention of Mary Magdalene, who will play such an important role at the climax of the story.

Mary Magdalene

Finally comes the most shocking thing of all: Jesus' resurrection, the central event of human history, is revealed first not to his disciples, and not to the chief priests or the Roman governor, but to a group of women who came to attend to his body. Tradition names twelve men as the *apostles*, the ones Jesus sent out to convert the world —

or thirteen, if we count both Judas, who betrayed Jesus, and Matthias, who replaced him. Paul, specially chosen by Christ on the road to Damascus, also earns the rare title "Apostle." But only one person in history has ever been called "apostle to the apostles" — and that is St. Mary Magdalene, who has had that name in Church tradition at least since the Middle Ages. She was the one who brought the news of the Resurrection to the incredulous Eleven.

At a time when a woman's testimony was inadmissible in a court of law, it must have seemed almost perverse for Jesus to trust that news to a female. Certainly the pagans thought so: our old friend Celsus makes a lot of it. He can't conceal his contempt for people who would accept the witness of a mere woman:

> You say that, although he couldn't help himself when he was living, he rose after he was dead, and he showed the marks of his punishment and his hands that had been pierced on the cross.

> But who was it who saw this? Some crazy woman, as you admit, or someone else from the same magical sect....

> Is it credible that Christ, when he was alive, openly announced to everyone what he was — but when it became necessary that he should gain a strong belief in his resurrection from the dead, he should only show himself secretly to one woman and to his associates?[1]

But God doesn't make the same distinctions we make. Jesus spent his whole earthly ministry teaching us that lesson. He would talk to a Samaritan woman and shock his disciples — both because she needed to learn from him and because his disciples needed to be shocked. The world was turned upside down when the Messiah came, and in this topsy-turvy world Samaritans had something to teach Jews, and ordinary women, with no family connections, were worth as much as queens — no, as much as kings.

It's not surprising, then, that so many of Christ's first followers were women. And as his apostles spread his message through the world, women continued to be among the earliest and most enthusiastic listeners.

Lydia and the Helpers of Paul

Like Christ himself, St. Paul was willing to speak directly to women in spite of custom and prejudice; and also like Christ, he found that women were some of the chief supporters of his ministry. One of those women was Lydia, whom we meet in the Acts of the Apostles.

Lydia was Paul's first European convert, which in itself would be quite a distinction. She heard Paul's preaching in Philippi, then the biggest city in ancient Macedonia (Philippi's ruins are now in northeastern Greece), and she was so impressed that she begged Paul and his party to come stay with her. Notice, incidentally, that St. Luke was an eyewitness of these events — at this point, he was traveling with Paul:

> Setting sail therefore from Troas, we made a direct voyage to Samothrace, and the following day to Neapolis, and from there to Philippi, which is the leading city of the district of Macedonia, and a Roman colony. We remained in this city some days; and on the sabbath day

we went outside the gate to the riverside, where we supposed there was a place of prayer; and we sat down and spoke to the women who had come together. One who heard us was a woman named Lydia, from the city of Thyatira, a seller of purple goods, who was a worshiper of God. The Lord opened her heart to listen to what was said by Paul. And when she was baptized, with her household, she begged us, saying, "If you have judged me to be faithful to the Lord, come to my house and stay." And she prevailed upon us.

— Acts 16:11-15

Lydia was a "seller of purple goods," which probably made her quite a wealthy member of the merchant classes. "Purple" was the very expensive Tyrian purple dye used as a mark of rank for the highest classes. A child of the emperor was said to be "born in the purple," the same way we might say that a child was born with a silver spoon in his mouth.

We notice one interesting aspect of Paul's preaching in this incident. Paul and his friends preached without hesitation to women. They didn't wait for their husbands or fathers to arrive; they talked to the women themselves. We can tell that Paul took it seriously when he said "there is neither male nor female." Once again, it's hard for us to imagine how revolutionary that was, but the New Testament is practically the first time we hear of any such thing — a man with a message going out to preach to women — in the whole history of the ancient world.

Women like Lydia made up a large part of the very early Church. The whole last chapter of Paul's letter to the Romans is a series of greetings to his friends, and we can't help noticing how many of them are women. First, he tells his Roman friends to accept "our sister Phoebe" and "help her in whatever she may require from you" (Romans 16:1-2). Apparently, Phoebe was someone who could take charge of a situation and get things done: she's called a "deaconess," which is Greek for "helper." Then Paul conveys his greetings to many others by name, and — once again — it's worth noticing that he doesn't distinguish between men and women.

We see the same thing in other letters from Paul. Priscilla (or Prisca, of which "Priscilla" is an affectionate diminutive) and her husband Aquila are greeted by name in three different letters; in two of them, Paul mentions Priscilla's name first (Romans 16:3 and 2 Timothy 4:19), and in one, Aquila's (1 Corinthians 16:19), as if neither one was in any way more important to him than the other.

Together with the Acts of the Apostles, these letters of Paul give us a picture of a Church that was unlike any other organization in its day. We don't see ordained women, but we do see women doing every other job in the Church. If women are getting work done, then the rest of the brethren are supposed to give them the help they need and follow their example.

The Church was the *only* place where women had that kind of respect: they were people, they were important, and they were appreciated. For that reason, they were probably also a majority of the Christian converts. The growth of Christianity is an interesting sociological phenomenon: it shows us what happens to a culture that treats one sex with careless contempt or even hostility. Pagan families often got rid of girl children; Christian families treasured girl children and often adopted abandoned girls. And women were converting to Christianity at an even faster clip than men. The predictable effect was that, after a while, there was a serious shortage of pagan women. Pagan men married Christian women, and the husbands were often converted by their wives — or even if the husbands didn't convert, their wives made sure that the children were raised Christian.[2]

And that sociological fact is one of the things that account for the strange anomaly of the persecuted Church: when the Church was despised, illegal, and persecuted — when it was death to be denounced as a Christian — the numbers of Christians were growing exponentially.

Dark times were coming. The age of martyrdom was at hand. And, once again, it would be the women of the Church who would astonish the world with their courage and conviction.

Chapter 3

Martyrs and Heroines

It took real courage to be a Christian in the early years. Almost as soon as the Roman government learned that there were such things as Christians, the persecutions started. And one of the most unexpected places we find records of great Christian women is in the lives of the martyrs. It may not seem terribly surprising to us moderns, but when we think of what a woman was in the pagan world, it's simply astonishing. Like anybody else, these Christians were telling stories of great heroes who died in battle. But their most popular heroes were women!

Christians taught in words, but more powerfully in deeds. The ultimate deed, in every sense, was martyrdom, and Christians knew that their deaths were preaching the

Gospel. The very word *martyr* means "witness": a martyr was showing the world what it meant to be a Christian.

Pagans had their martyrs too, but they were seldom martyrs of faith. The tragic heroes of pagan history were almost never men who died for their gods, and almost always men who died for their country. "*Dulce et decorum est pro patria mori*," the Roman poet Horace said: "It is sweet and proper to die for your country." No one died for Mercury or Minerva.

Christians, however, were martyred *by* their country, not for it. Considering what they suffered, they showed surprising patriotism: they always prayed for the emperor, even when the emperor was using them as human torches for his garden parties. But their country was not what they died for: they were citizens of heaven more than of any earthly empire.

The other obvious difference is that pagan heroes were almost always men. No poet wrote twenty-four books on the heroic deeds of a twelve-year-old girl. There were some strong women in pagan literature, of course. Dido in the Aeneid is a beautifully drawn and tragic character. In the larger story, however, she's nothing but a trap. If Aeneas stays to enjoy her company, he won't found Rome. He has to get away from her, because he's the hero, not she, and it just won't do for him to stick around. In fact, she's a danger precisely because she's strong and intelligent, not submissive and rather stupid the way she ought to be. There's no room for her in an epic hero's life.

But the Christians actually made women themselves their epic heroes. Stories of Sts. Perpetua and Felicity, of St. Agnes, and of Proba were told over and over again as examples of courage and tenacity. In the upside-down, inside-out world of the Christians, the hero was not a man who flashed his sword in battle, but a woman who just stood there and accepted death for the sake of Christ.

In all the lives of the early martyrs, there's not one instance of a Christian deciding that, if he was going to die, he was going to take a bunch of pagans with him. That's what made these stories so hard to understand for a well-educated pagan. Homer, with his endless battles and lovingly detailed descriptions of intestines pouring out on the ground, was the closest thing Greek and Roman pagans had to a canonical scripture. How could anyone admire these people who just stood and waited to be executed like common criminals? They didn't even try to fight back! This Christian idea of virtue was almost, well, womanly!

But the ordinary Roman in the street seemed to get the idea quickly. Conversions multiplied, and the enthusiastic converts repeated the stories of the glorious martyrs over and over.

One kind of heroine that keeps popping up in these Christian adventure stories is the consecrated virgin. Often the young woman defies her parents' demand that she marry some rich wastrel. She may go to martyrdom, as Agnes of Rome did. She may live happily ever after (with some colorful adventures along the way), as Thecla did. But the important thing is that she makes her own choice.

It's hard for us, in our day of legal equality between the sexes, to imagine how revolutionary these Christian virgins were. The choice of Christian virginity gave a woman a power nothing else in the ancient world gave her. It gave her the right to be defined as a *person*, not as a man's possession. She belonged to Christ alone, and in Christ there is neither male nor female: "You are Christ's, and Christ is God's" (1 Corinthians 3:23). It's no wonder so many women of all classes chose this way of life: even for a noble-woman from a rich family, it might be the only way to be *herself* — to make a choice about what was really important in her life.

ST. THECLA

The story of Thecla (first century) comes to us from a book called the *Acts of Paul and Thecla*. It seems to have been written in Greek, but we also have it in Coptic, Ethiopian, and Syriac translations. It may have been part of a longer apocryphal *Acts of Paul*, but the story of Thecla is satis-fyingly complete in itself, and it concentrates on Thecla rather than on St. Paul.

This is a controversial book, and it always has been. Writing in about the year 190, Tertullian claims that it was a recent forgery:

> If certain Acts of Paul (falsely so called) defend the ex-ample of Thecla in giving women license to teach and baptize, be it known that, in Asia, the priest who put together that writing, thinking he would add to Paul's reputation, was discovered and removed from his place, having confessed that he did it out of love for Paul.
>
> — *ANF* 3:677

Tertullian was no fan of women as teachers: he thought they should not teach at all. (This is not the view of the Catholic Church, by the way, which has named women among the Doctors of the Church: that is, the saints whose teachings are regarded as extraordinarily useful to the Church.) We might call him an extremist, in this and in some other matters.

But his evidence is interesting not just because he says the *Acts of Paul and Thecla* is a forgery, but because he proves that it's a very early writing, even if it is a forgery. It had to have been written within a century of the time of the apostles, because Tertullian himself was writing within a century of the time of the apostles.

At any rate, Tertullian's opinion was not shared by everyone. We know that some version of the *Acts* was being read in public at Thecla's memorial two hundred years after Tertullian's time. The general opinion among early Christians seems to have been that, even if the text itself was not completely reliable, the story of Thecla was mainly true.

The author of the *Acts of Paul and Thecla* seems to have been influenced by Gnostic heresies. In particular, the text is strongly against marriage and puts extreme ideas of chastity into Paul's mouth.

Some modern writers call it a "novel" or "romance," but that's an anachronistic way of looking at it. A Christian storyteller would sit down to write a story that he *believed* was true — he wouldn't just make it up. Most likely, the story is based on real tradition, with some exaggeration and filling in of details.

And it seems beyond all doubt that Thecla existed: the tradition of the Church is unanimous, and churches have been dedicated to her since very early times.

How much of the rest is true is endlessly debatable, but that's almost beside the point. What's important to us is what her story says about the early Christians' idea of women.

According to the story, Thecla defied her parents, defied her betrothed, defied the nobility, refused to marry, chose to answer Christ's call, and lived to an advanced age in spite of many perilous adventures. She tossed all the traditional male authority figures aside and made her own way in the world. She even cut her hair and dressed in men's clothes so that she could go out looking for Paul.

And this was the role model for Christian women across the Roman Empire! No wonder the pagan traditionalists were so upset. Christianity really was destroying Roman family values.

So here's the story of Thecla, the way the Christians told it for centuries, and the way it inspired generations of young Christian women to make up their minds for themselves.

Thecla Rejects Her Betrothed

The story begins in the way many secular romances begin, with a beautiful young woman falling in love. But Thecla falls in love, not with a handsome young man, but with Christian teaching. The story makes a point of telling us that she never saw what Paul even looked like; she only heard what he said, and she was captivated by it.

While Paul was speaking in the church in the house of Onesiphorus, there was a certain virgin named Thecla who was sitting at the window nearby. She was the daughter of Theocleia and betrothed to a man named Thamyris.

Thecla listened night and day while Paul talked about virginity and prayer. She never looked away from the window but — with great joy — paid close attention to the faith. And when she saw many women going in beside Paul, she, too, had an earnest desire to be deemed worthy to stand in Paul's presence and to hear the word of Christ — for she had never seen what he looked like, but only heard what he said.

Now, because she would not leave the window, her mother sent for Thamyris. He came gladly, as if he were already receiving her in marriage.

Theocleia said, "I have a strange story to tell you, Thamyris. For three days and three nights, Thecla has not left the window. She doesn't eat or drink; she just looks intently, as if she saw some pleasant sight. She is so devoted to some foreigner with his lying and crafty teachings that I wonder how a virgin of such modesty can be so completely taken in. Thamyris, this man will overthrow the city of the Iconians — and your Thecla too. All the women and the young men are going in with him, and he teaches them to fear God and live in chastity. And my daughter, tied to the window like a spider, lays hold of what Paul says with a strange eagerness and terrible emotion. The girl looks eagerly at what he says, and she has been spellbound. You go to her and speak to her, since she's been betrothed to you."

Thamyris went to her and kissed her, though at the same time he was afraid of her overpowering emotion.

"Thecla, my betrothed," he said, "why are you sitting here this way? Turn around to your Thamyris and come to your senses."

Her mother said the same things too. "Why are you sitting here looking down like that, my child? Why don't you answer? Why do you just sit like a mad woman?"

They wept dreadfully — Thamyris, for the loss of a wife; Theocleia, for the loss of a child; the maidservants, for the loss of a mistress. There was much confusion in the house of mourning.

But while all this was going on, Thecla did not turn around but kept listening earnestly to what Paul said.

Thamyris stood up and went out into the street, where he kept an eye on everyone who was going in to Paul and coming out. And he saw two men arguing fiercely with each other. "Gentlemen," he said, "tell me who this is among you who's leading the souls of young men astray and deceiving virgins so that they do not marry but remain as they are. If you tell me about him, I promise to give you plenty of money — I'm the most important man in the city."

Demas and Ermogenes said to him, "We don't really know who this is, but he deprives young men of wives, and girls of husbands, by saying, 'There is no resurrection for you unless you remain chaste, and do not pollute the flesh, but keep it chaste.' "

"Come to my house," Thamyris said to them, "and rest yourselves."

They went to a lavish dinner, with lots of wine, great wealth, and a splendid table. Thamyris made them drink, because he was in love with Thecla and wanted to get her as his wife.

During the dinner, Thamyris said, "Gentlemen, tell me, what is his teaching? Tell me, so I may also know. I'm worried a lot about Thecla, because she loves the foreigner so much, and I can't marry her."

Demas and Ermogenes said, "Bring him before the governor Castelios on the charge of persuading the mob to take up the new teaching of the Christians. He'll destroy him quickly, and you'll have Thecla as your wife. And we'll teach you that the resurrection of which this man speaks has already happened, because it has already happened in the children we have, and we rose again when we came to the knowledge of the true God."

Hearing these things, Thamyris was filled with anger and rage. He got up early and went to the house of Onesiphorus with magistrates and public officers and a great crowd with batons, saying, "You have corrupted the city of the Iconians, and the woman who was betrothed to me. Now she won't have me. Come with us to the governor Castelios."

And the mob said, "Away with the magician! He has corrupted all our wives, and the multitudes have been persuaded to change their beliefs."

In front of the tribunal, Thamyris said, with a great shout, "Proconsul! This man — we don't know who he is — makes virgins unwilling to marry! Make him say before you why he teaches these things."

Demas and Ermogenes said to Thamyris, "Say that he's a Christian, and you'll get rid of him that way."

But the proconsul prevented that: he called Paul, saying, "Who are you, and what do you teach? These are not trivial charges they bring against you."

Paul lifted up his voice and said, "Since today I am examined on what I teach, listen, proconsul: A living God — a God of retributions — a jealous God — a God who needs nothing, planning to save humanity — has sent me to reclaim humanity from corruption and uncleanness, and pleasure, and death, so that they will not sin. Therefore God sent his own Son, whom I preach, and in whom I teach people to place their hope — he alone has compassion on a world led astray — so that they will not be under judgment anymore, proconsul, but will have faith, the fear of God, the knowledge of holiness, and the love of truth. So if I teach what has been revealed to me by God, what am I doing that's wrong?"

When the proconsul heard that, he ordered Paul to be bound and sent to prison — "until I have the time to hear him more attentively."

At night, Thecla took off her bracelets and gave them to the gatekeeper. He opened the door for her. She went into the prison and gave the jailer a silver mirror. Then she went in where Paul was and, sitting at his feet, heard the great things of God. Paul feared nothing but confidently left his life in God's care. And her faith was increased as well. She kissed his fetters.

Thecla's friends were looking for her, and Thamyris was running up and down the streets as if she were lost.

One of the gatekeeper's fellow slaves told Thamyris that she had gone out in the middle of the night. So they went out and questioned the gatekeeper, and he said, "She's gone to the foreigner in the prison."

So they went there and found her, chained by affection, so to speak.

They went out and got the mob together and told the governor what had happened. He ordered Paul to be brought to the tribunal. Thecla was sitting on the ground where Paul was sitting and teaching her in the prison, and the governor ordered her to be brought to the tribunal as well. She came out with all the signs of joy.

When Paul had been brought out, the crowd shouted vehemently, "He's a magician! Take him away!"

But the proconsul gladly heard Paul speak about the holy works of Christ.

He called a council and summoned Thecla, saying, "Why don't you obey Thamyris, according to the law of the Iconians?"

But she stood looking earnestly at Paul.

When she would not answer, her mother cried out, "Burn the wicked wretch! She refuses to marry — burn her in the middle of the theater! Then all the women who have been taught by this man will be afraid."

The governor was greatly moved. He scourged Paul and threw him out of the city, and he condemned Thecla to be burned. The governor went straight to the theater, and the whole crowd went out to the spectacle of Thecla's execution.

But as a lamb in the wilderness looks around for the shepherd, so she kept searching for Paul. And looking at the crowd, she saw the Lord sitting in the likeness of Paul, and she said, "Since I can't endure my fate, Paul has come to see me." And she gazed on him with great earnestness, and he went up to heaven.

The maidservants and virgins brought the wood to burn Thecla. And when she came in naked, the governor wept and marveled at the power that was in her.

The public executioners piled up the wood and arranged it so she could go up to the top of the pile. She made the sign of the cross and climbed up the pile. Then they set fire to it.

Though a great fire was blazing, it did not touch her. God had compassion on her; he made a rumbling under the ground, and a cloud overshadowed them from above, full of rain and hail; and everything in the hollow of the cloud was poured out, so that many were in danger of death. The fire was put out, and Thecla was saved.

— ACTS OF PAUL AND THECLA, 2-5

Thecla Faces the Beasts

From here, Thecla goes with Paul to Antioch. She wants to be baptized right away, but Paul tells her to wait: the proper time will come.

In Antioch, Thecla begins her next adventure by beating up a nobleman who tried to rape her. Here, not only Thecla herself but the women of the city as well are shown as rebelling against the wicked exercise of power by the nobleman and the corrupt governor.

A certain Syrian nobleman by the name of Alexander fell in love with Thecla when he saw her and tried to win Paul over with gifts and presents.

But Paul said, "I don't know the woman you're talking about. She doesn't belong to me."

But Alexander was a very powerful man, so he embraced her in the street. She would not stand for it; she looked around for Paul. And she cried out bitterly, "Don't force a stranger! Don't force the servant of God! I'm one of the chief people in Iconia, and I've been thrown out of the city because I wouldn't have Thamyris."

And she took hold of Alexander and tore his cloak and pulled off his crown. She made him a laughingstock.

He still loved her, but at the same time he was ashamed of what had happened. He brought her before the governor. She confessed that she had done these things, and he condemned her to the wild beasts.

The women were astonished. "Evil judgment!" they cried out beside the tribunal. "Impious judgment!"

Thecla asked the governor, "Let me remain pure until I fight the wild beasts."

A certain Tryphaena, whose daughter was dead, took her into her house and consoled herself with her company.

When it came time for the beast show, they bound Thecla to a fierce lioness, and Tryphaena accompanied her. But the lioness, with Thecla sitting on her, licked her feet. The whole crowd was astonished.

The charge on her inscription was "Sacrilege." And the women cried out from above, "An impious judgment has been passed in this city!"

After the show, Tryphaena took Thecla back again, for her daughter Falconilla had died and said to her in a dream: "Mother, you shall have this stranger Thecla in my place, so that she may pray for me, and I may be transferred to the place of the righteous."

So when Tryphaena took her back home after the show, she grieved that she would have to fight the wild beasts the next day. She loved her as much as her daughter Falconilla.

"My second child Thecla," she said, "come and pray for my child, so that she may live forever. For I saw this in my sleep."

Thecla did not hesitate at all. She lifted up her voice and said, "God most high, grant this woman her wish, that her daughter Falconilla may live forever."

And when Thecla had said that, Tryphaena wept that so much beauty had to be thrown to the wild beasts.

When it was dawn, Alexander came to take her, for he was the one who gave the hunt. "The governor is sitting," he said, "and the crowd is in an uproar against us. Let me take her away to fight the wild beasts."

And Tryphaena cried out, so loud that even Alexander fled: "A second mourning for my Falconilla has come upon my house, and there is no one to help! No child — she's dead. No relative — I'm a widow. God of Thecla, help her!"

The governor sent an order that Thecla should be brought at once. And Tryphaena, taking her by the hand, said, "I took my daughter Falconilla to the tomb, and I'm taking you, Thecla, to fight the wild beasts."

Thecla wept bitterly saying, "Lord, the God in whom I believe, to whom I fled for refuge, who delivered me from the fire, grant a compensation to Tryphaena, who has had compassion on your servant and has kept me pure."

Then there was an uproar. The crowd cried out, "Away with this sacrilegious woman!" But the women, all sitting together, were saying, "Let the city rise up against this wickedness! Take us all off, proconsul! Cruel sight! Evil sentence!"

Thecla was taken from Tryphaena's arms and stripped. She was given a girdle and thrown into the arena. Lions and bears and a fierce lioness were let loose on her.

The lioness ran up to her feet and lay down, and all the women cried out. And a bear ran at her — but the lioness met the bear and tore it to pieces. Again, a lion that had been trained against men (it belonged to Alexander) ran at her. The lioness fought against the lion and was killed along with him. The women made great lamentation, seeing that her protector the lioness was dead.

After that they sent in many wild beasts. Thecla stood and stretched forth her hands, praying. When she had finished her prayer, she turned and saw a ditch full of water, and said, "Now it is time to wash myself." And she threw herself in, saying, "In the name of Jesus Christ I am baptized on my last day."

The women saw what she was doing, and the whole crowd too, and they wept. "Don't throw yourself into the water!" they said. And the governor shed tears, too, because the seals were going to devour such beauty.

She threw herself in, in the name of Jesus Christ. But the seals had seen the glare of the lightning-fire, and they floated dead on the water. There was a cloud of fire around her, so that the wild beasts could not touch her, and she could not be seen naked.

The women wailed when other wild beasts were thrown in. And some of them threw sweet herbs, and others threw nard and cinnamon and cardamom, so that there was perfume everywhere. And all the wild beasts that had been thrown in did not touch her, as if they had been held back by sleep.

Now Alexander said to the governor, "I have some extraordinarily terrible bulls; since she is condemned to fight the beasts, let us bind her to them."

The governor, looking gloomy, turned and said, "Do what you like."

They bound her by the feet between the bulls and put red-hot irons to the bulls' private parts, so that they might be made more furious and kill her.

But Tryphaena fainted beside the arena, so that the crowd said, "Queen Tryphaena is dead!"

The governor halted the games, and the city was in dismay.

Alexander begged the governor, "Have mercy both on me and on the city, and release this woman! If Caesar hears of these things, he'll quickly destroy the city and us as well, because his relative Queen Tryphaena has died beside the Abaci."

The governor summoned Thecla out of the midst of the wild beasts, and said to her, "Who are you? And what is there about you that not one of the wild beasts touches you?"

"I am a servant of the living God," she said, "and as for what there is about me, I have believed in the Son of God, in whom he is well pleased. For that reason, not one of the beasts has touched me. He alone is the end of salvation and the basis of immortal life. He is a refuge to the tempest-tossed, a comfort to the afflicted, a shelter to the despairing. Once and for all, whoever does not believe in him will not live forever."

When the governor had heard this, he ordered her clothes to be brought and put on her. Thecla said, "He who clothed me when I was naked among the wild beasts will clothe you with salvation in the day of judgment."

Therefore the governor immediately issued an edict: "I release to you the God-fearing Thecla, the servant of God."

The women shouted aloud, and with one voice they gave thanks to God, saying, "There is one God, the God of Thecla!" And the foundations of the theater were shaken by their voice.

When Tryphaena heard the good news, she went to meet the holy Thecla, and said, "Now I believe that the dead are raised. Now I believe that my child lives. Come in, and I'll give you everything that's mine."

So she went along with her and rested eight days, and she taught her in the word of God, so that even most of the maidservants believed. And there was great joy in the house.

— ACTS OF PAUL AND THECLA, 7-9

ST. PERPETUA AND ST. FELICITY

Perpetua (d. 203) is almost unique among the martyrs because she wrote the story of her own martyrdom — or, rather, she wrote everything up to the martyrdom itself, "but as for what happens in the games, let anyone who wants to write that."

Perpetua was a noblewoman who lived in Carthage, a great city in Africa (it's now a suburb of Tunis, the capital city of Tunisia). Felicity (d. 203) was her slave. They were recent converts to Christianity, and that was their crime: the emperor Septimius Severus wasn't persecuting Christians per se at the moment, but he had made it a capital crime for Roman citizens to become Jews or Christians. In the early 200s, they were sentenced to be thrown to the beasts. Even though Perpetua was nursing a baby and Felicity was pregnant, the court showed them no mercy — or, rather, from the judge's point of view, the court showed extraordinary mercy. The women could walk out free at any moment if they would only renounce their silly cult. But they stubbornly refused.

Perpetua's Vision

The day before she was scheduled to go into the arena, Perpetua had this vivid dream in which, instead of being

thrown to the beasts, she fought in the arena — and won —
as a gladiator. The most remarkable thing about her dream
is that she sees herself turned into a man. The symbolism of
the vision seems clear: in martyrdom, a Christian woman is
no longer a woman, as the world sees a woman — that is,
she is no longer defined by her "weakness" and "dependence."
Instead, she takes on a role the world thinks is reserved for
men: the role of conquering hero.

The day before we were going to fight, I saw in a vision that Pomponius the deacon had come here to the door of the prison and knocked on it hard. I went out to him and opened it for him; he was wearing a white robe with no belt and curiously wrought shoes.

He said to me, "Perpetua, we're waiting for you. Come."

And he took my hand, and we began to go through rugged and winding places. At last, with much heavy breathing, we came to the amphitheater, and he led me into the midst of the arena.

And he said to me, "Don't be afraid. I'm here with you, and I'm laboring together with you." Then he went away.

I saw many people watching closely. And because I knew that I was condemned to the beasts, I was surprised that beasts were not sent out against me.

Then a certain ugly Egyptian, with his helpers, came out against me to fight with me. There also came to me handsome young men, my helpers and assistants. And I was stripped naked, and I became a man. My helpers began to rub me with oil as their custom is for a contest; and on the other side I saw that Egyptian wallowing in the dust.

And there came forth a man of very great stature, so that he was taller than the very top of the amphitheater, wearing a robe without a belt, and beneath it, between the two stripes over the breast, a robe of purple; having also shoes curiously wrought in gold and silver; bearing a rod like a master of gladiators and a green branch on which there were golden apples. He asked for silence and said, "If the Egyptian conquers this woman, he shall slay her with the sword; and if she conquers him, she shall receive this branch." Then he went away.

We came near each other and began to strike each other. He tried to trip up my feet, but I kicked his face with my heels. And I rose up into the air and began to kick him as if I weren't bound to the earth. But when I saw that there was still some delay, I joined my hands with the fingers intertwined. I grabbed his head, and he fell on his face, and I trod upon his head.

The people began to shout, and my helpers began to sing. And I went up to the master of gladiators and received the branch. And he kissed me and said to me, "Daughter, peace be with you." And I began to go with glory to the gate called the Gate of Life.

Then I woke up, and I understood that I would not be fighting with beasts but against the devil; but I knew that victory would be mine.

So far I have written this, till the day before the games; but as for what happens in the games, let anyone who wants to write that.[3]

— *ANF* 3:72

The Martyrdom of Perpetua and Felicity

Someone else did indeed take up a pen to record the events of the next day, so we have an eyewitness account of Perpetua's martyrdom in the arena.

Throwing criminals to the beasts was intended to provide entertainment to the jaded populace, although the authorities doubtless justified it by telling themselves that it was making a public example of dangerous criminals. It was a horrible and barbaric entertainment, but Perpetua, Felicity, and their companions seem to have entered into the spirit of the thing and turned it on its head. The judge wanted a public spectacle? Fine, he would have a public spectacle. But it would be a spectacle of courage and purity. The slobbering spectators would be forced to watch, not criminals begging for their lives, but witnesses to Christ dying on their own terms. The martyrs were acutely aware that everything they did in their last minutes was done in the public eye, and they were determined to make their deaths instructive.

Now shone the day of their victory, and they went forth from prison into the amphitheater as if they were going to heaven, joyful and bright-faced. If they did tremble, it was with joy, not with fear.

Perpetua walked on brightly, as a matron of Christ, as one pleasing to God, averting the brightness of her eyes from everyone's sight; and Felicity, too, rejoicing that she had delivered her child so that she might battle against the beasts, from blood to blood, from midwife to battle, washing after the birth with a second baptism.

They were led to the gate and were ordered to put on the costumes: the men, the garb of priests of Saturn; and the women, that sacred to Ceres. But the noble woman resisted right to the end with firmness. She said, "For this reason we have willingly come through this far, so that our liberty might not be curbed. For this reason we have yielded our spirits, so that we would not have to do anything like this. This was the agreement we made with you."

Injustice acknowledged the justice. The tribune conceded that they could be led in simply as they were.

Perpetua sang psalms, already trampling the head of the Egyptian. Revocatus, Saturninus, and Saturus threatened the spectators about this.

When they came under the gaze of Hilarianus, they began to say to him, with gesture and nod, "You judge us, but God judges you."[4]

At this, the people, exasperated, demanded that they be beaten with scourges along the line of the beast-wranglers. And they certainly did rejoice that they should follow in even one of the Lord's passions.

But he who said, "Ask and you shall receive," gave all of them the deaths they had longed for.

When they had been talking among themselves about what they wanted in their martyrdom, Saturninus proclaimed that he wanted to be thrown to all the beasts, obviously so that he might wear a more glorious crown. Thus, in the beginning of the show, he and Revocatus endured the leopard, and on the scaffold they were attacked by the bear.

Saturus, on the other hand, thought nothing was more abominable than a bear, but supposed that he might be finished off by one bite of the leopard. Thus, when a wild boar was brought in, it was the wrangler who brought it that was gored by the beast; he died after the day of the show. Saturus was simply dragged away. And when he was bound on the floor near a bear, the bear would not come out of its den. Thus, Saturus was brought back uninjured a second time.

For the young women, on the other hand, the devil prepared a very ferocious cow, contrary to established custom, rivaling their sex among the beasts. They were thus led forth stripped and draped in nets.

The people shuddered, gazing on one delicate young woman and another with breasts still dripping from her recent delivery.

Thus they were called back in and unbound. First Perpetua was thrown, and she fell on her loins. And when she saw her tunic torn from her side, she pulled it back to cover her thigh — her modesty rather than her pain uppermost in her mind. After that she was called in again, and she pinned up her straying hair — for it was not becoming to a martyr to suffer with unkempt hair, which might make her seem to be mourning in her glory. Thus she stood up.

And when she saw Felicity trampled, she went to her, offered her hand, and raised her. And both of them stood together. And when the hardness of the people was subdued, they were recalled to the Sanavivaria gate.

There Perpetua was met by a certain man named Rusticus, who was at that time a catechumen. He stayed by her. And as if she had woken from sleep — so far had she been in the Spirit and in ecstasy — she started to look around, and to everyone's amazement she said, "When will we be led out to that cow? I don't know."

And when she heard what had already happened, at first she did not believe it, until she recognized some of the signs of injury in her body and dress.

Then she called her brother and that catechumen to her and spoke to them, saying, "Stick to your faith, and every one of you love one another, and don't be scandalized by our sufferings."

Meanwhile Saturus, at the other gate, exhorted the soldier Prudentius, saying, "Certainly I am at the peak, just as I promised and predicted. Right to this very moment I have felt no beast. And now believe with all your heart. I'm going out there, and I'll be consumed with one bite of the leopard."

And right at the end of the show, he was thrown to the leopard. And with one bite he was bathed with so much blood that the people, as he was returning, shouted the testimony of his second baptism: "Saved and washed! Saved and washed!"

Plainly he must certainly have been saved, if he was washed that way.

Then Saturus said to the soldier Prudentius, "Farewell. Remember my faith. And do not let these things confuse you but confirm you." And at the same time, Saturus asked for a ring from Prudentius' finger, and having dipped it in his blood, returned it to him as an inheritance, leaving him a pledge and a memorial of his blood. And after that, he was dropped lifeless on the ground with the rest, to have his throat cut in the usual place.

The people called for them to be brought back in, so that when the sword penetrated their bodies they could make their eyes partners in the murder. Then they stood up on the other side and moved to where the people wanted them. But first they kissed one another in turn, so that they might consummate their martyrdom with the kiss of peace.

The others were immobile and silent as the iron pierced them — Saturus all the more: he had also gone up the ladder first and given up his spirit, for he was also sustaining Perpetua.

Perpetua, on the other hand, so that she might taste some suffering, was pierced between the ribs and cried out. And she herself brought the hand of the inexperienced gladiator to her throat.

Probably a woman like that, who was feared by the foul spirit, could not have been killed unless she herself had willed it.

— *ANF* 3:704-705

ST. BLANDINA

Blandina (d. 177) was a slave girl whose owner was a Christian woman in Lyons. When mob violence against the Christians turned into official persecution, there were many who lost their lives — but Blandina was remembered as the chief inspiration. The Christians who survived the persecution saw in her an example of Christ's saying that the last would be made first in his kingdom.

Accused of Cannibalism

Cannibalism was a common accusation against the early Christians. It sounds ridiculous, but it's easy to see how the rumors got started. Christians would not reveal the details of the Eucharist to anyone who was not baptized. But their servants or neighbors might overhear something about eating Christ's flesh and drinking his blood. What is this awful secret the Christians are keeping? Something about eating flesh and drinking blood! St. Irenaeus sets up our story by telling us how easily those very rumors got started in one famous case. What's true now was true then as well: If you extract information from someone by torture, it's very likely to be the wrong information.

St. Irenaeus was bishop of Lyons (Lugdunum, or Lyons in modern French) when the mob violence against the Christians broke out, so he gives us eyewitness testimony. The prefect sided with the mob, and as an "entertainment" decided to give a public spectacle of Christians being devoured by wild animals.

The Greeks arrested the slaves of Christian catechumens and then used force against them to learn some secret of Christian practice. These slaves had nothing to say that would please their tormentors, except that they had heard from their masters that the divine Communion was the body and blood of Christ and, imagining that it was actually flesh and blood, gave their inquisitors that answer. The torturers assumed that this was what Christian practice was and gave that information to other Greeks. They tried to force the martyrs Sanctus and Blandina to confess to it under the influence of torture. Blandina very admirably replied to these men, "How could they endure such a thing, when, for the sake of their practice, they won't even touch the meat that is permitted?"

— *ANF* 1:570

The Martyrdom of Blandina

Now that we've heard the background from Irenaeus, we turn to the historian Eusebius for a detailed account of the martyrdom of Blandina. Though the prefect had hoped to discourage Christians by showing them a terrible public punishment, Christian men and women looked at Blandina and saw an image of Christ on the cross. Some who had renounced their Christianity to save their lives saw her bravery and renounced their renouncements, cheerfully following where the lowly slave girl Blandina led.

The people were furious with Sanctus, the deacon from Vienne; and Maturus, a recent convert but a noble fighter; and Attalus, a native of Pergamos, where he had always been a pillar and a foundation; and Blandina, through whom Christ showed that things that look low and obscure and contemptible to us are very glorious to God by means of love for him shown in power and not boasting in appearance.

While we were all trembling, and while her earthly mistress, who was also one of the witnesses, feared that she would not be able to make a bold confession because her body was so weak, Blandina was filled with such power that she was delivered from and raised above those who were torturing her, one after another, from morning to evening, in every way. They admitted they were beaten, and they could do nothing more to her. And they were amazed at her endurance, since her whole body was mangled and broken. They testified that one of these forms of torture was enough to kill her, let alone so many sufferings and so great.

But the blessed woman, like a noble athlete, renewed her strength in her confession. Her comfort, diversion, and relief from the pain of her sufferings were in exclaiming, "I am a Christian! We do nothing vile!"

… Maturus, Sanctus, Blandina, and Attalus were therefore led to the amphitheater to be exposed to the wild beasts and to give the heathen public a spectacle of cruelty, a day for fighting with wild beasts being specially appointed on account of our people.

Both Maturus and Sanctus passed again through every torment in the amphitheater, as if they had suffered nothing before — or rather, as if, having already conquered their antagonist in many contests, they were now striving for the crown itself. They endured again the customary running of the gauntlet and the violence of the wild beasts, and everything the furious people called for or desired, and at last the iron chair in which their bodies were roasted and they were tormented with the fumes.

The persecutors did not stop at that but were yet more furious against them, determined to overcome their patience. But even so, they did not hear a word from Sanctus except the confession he had uttered from the beginning.

These four, then, after their life had continued for a long time through the great conflict, were at last sacrificed, having been made throughout that day a spectacle to the world, in place of the usual variety of combats.

Blandina was suspended on a stake and exposed to be devoured by the wild beasts that were to attack her. And because she appeared as if hanging on a cross, and because of her earnest prayers, she inspired the combatants with great zeal. They looked on her in her conflict and saw with their outward eyes, in the form of their sister, him who was crucified for them, that he might persuade those who believe in him that everyone who suffers for the glory of Christ has fellowship always with the living God.

None of the wild beasts touched her then, so she was taken down from the stake and thrown into prison again. She was preserved thus for another contest. By being victorious in more conflicts, she would make the punishment of the crooked serpent irrevocable. Though she was small and weak and despised, yet clothed with Christ the mighty and conquering Athlete, she would stir up the zeal of the brethren. When she had overcome the adversary many times, she would receive, through her conflict, the incorruptible crown....

But the intervening time was not wasted or fruitless to them, for by their patience the measureless compassion of Christ was shown. For through their continued life, the dead were made alive, and the witnesses showed favor to those who had failed to witness. And the virgin mother had much joy in receiving alive those whom she had brought forth as dead. For through their influence, many who had denied were restored, and re-begotten, and re-kindled with life, and learned to confess. And being made alive and strengthened, they went to the judgment seat to be again interrogated by the governor. God, who has no pleasure in the death of the wicked [see Ezekiel 33:11], but mercifully invites them to repentance, had treated them with kindness.

Caesar commanded that they should be put to death, but that any who might deny Christ should be set free. Therefore, at the beginning of the public festival that took place there, attended by crowds from all nations, the governor brought the blessed ones to the judgment seat, to make a show and spectacle out of them for the multitude. So he examined them again and beheaded those who appeared to possess Roman citizenship.[5] The others he sent to the wild beasts.

And Christ was glorified greatly in those who had formerly denied him, for, contrary to the expectation of the heathen, they confessed. For they were examined by themselves, as about to be set free; but confessing, they were added to the order of the witnesses. Some stayed outside, who had never possessed a trace of faith, or any apprehension of the wedding garment [see Matthew 22:11], or an understanding of the fear of God. As sons of perdition, they blasphemed the Way through their apostasy. But all the others were added to the Church....

On the last day of the contests, Blandina was again brought in, with Ponticus, a boy about fifteen years old.

They had been brought every day to witness the sufferings of the others and had been pressed to swear by the idols. But because they remained steadfast and despised them, the multitude became furious, so that they had no compassion for the youth of the boy or respect for the sex of the woman.

Therefore, they exposed them to all the terrible sufferings and took them through the entire round of torture, repeatedly urging them to swear. But they were unable to make them do it; for Ponticus, encouraged by his sister so that even the heathen could see that she was confirming and strengthening him, nobly endured every torture, and he then gave up the ghost.

But the blessed Blandina, last of all — after she had, like a noble mother, encouraged her children and sent them before her victorious to the King — endured all their conflicts herself, and hurried after them, glad and rejoicing in her departure as if called to a marriage supper, rather than cast to wild beasts.

— *NPNF2* 1:213-217

ST. AGNES OF ROME

Of all the ancient Christian martyrs, Agnes (d. c. 304) is probably the best documented. Within a few decades of her suffering, the heavyweights of Christian thought all had something to say about her: Ambrose, Augustine, Jerome, and Pope Damasus I, among others. There's no great Christian heroine better attested in history.

Yet we don't really know all that much about her, in spite of all those sources. There's no doubt about the central facts of the story, but the great writers who took up her cause were far more interested in her moral example than in detailed historical facts. What we do know is that Agnes was one of the most influential examples in Christian history. We also know that she was about twelve or thirteen years old when she was killed. That one detail is emphasized in every account of her martyrdom.

The outline of the story is this: Agnes was a beautiful young girl from a noble family. Admiring suitors were already besieging her: in imperial Rome, a pretty girl had to beat men away with a stick as soon as she showed the first signs of adolescence.

Agnes, however, had decided that only one bridegroom would do for her: she betrothed herself to Christ, and she would listen to no other appeals. Some frustrated and enraged suitor denounced her to the authorities as a Christian, and she was arrested.

Legend says that the judge, angered by her constant refusals to abjure her vow, sent her to a brothel to be corrupted. This is just the sort of thing a Roman judge would do. There were no long-term prisons in Roman law; a jail was a place where prisoners were kept only until they could be tried. Once they were tried, the judge had to decide what to do with them, making the punishment fit the crime as well as he could, often with a sadistic sense of whimsy. Women were often sent to brothels — and especially consecrated Christian virgins. It served them right for refusing to marry, which set a bad example for girls everywhere.

In the case of Agnes, however, her prayers kept her pure even in the brothel — whether by a miracle, as some later legends have it, or simply because she awed the customers with her piety and they refused to touch her (which would be a kind of miracle in itself). So she was brought back, tortured, and finally condemned to be executed in public, and she went to her death with cheerful courage.

The story of Agnes was more than the story of one brave young girl. Agnes came to stand for the sufferings of the countless Christian martyrs under Roman persecution — in just the same way that, centuries later, another young girl named Anne Frank would come to symbolize the sufferings of countless Jewish martyrs under Nazi persecution. And that may be the reason we don't have a complete and accurate account of her martyrdom.

This wonderfully brave girl was innocence and virtue incarnate, and her martyrdom, even as it was really happening, was already taking on symbolic and allegorical meanings. When Christians told her story, they didn't think about details of dates and names: they thought about innocence against oppression, virginity against depravity.

But the days of persecution were numbered. Was the death of Agnes the last straw? It may well have been. Here was the flower of Roman nobility, brutally killed by inflexible fanaticism. And she met her death bravely, with all the supposedly manly virtues that very few Roman men actually possessed. It may be that her death accomplished the one thing that really opened the door for Christianity in Rome: she finally made the pagans — the educated citizens who thought they were at the apex of civilization — ashamed of themselves.

At any rate, it was not long after Agnes died that Constantine conquered his rival under the banner of the cross, thus becoming the sole ruler of the western part of the Roman Empire. By that time she was already the Roman Christians' greatest popular heroine. Constantine's own daughter Constantina, or Constantia, built a great basilica just outside the walls of Rome, on the site of Agnes's tomb, a church that quickly became one of the greatest pilgrimage sites in the greatest city of the ancient world. That church — known as *Sant'Agnese fuori le Mura* (St. Agnes Outside the Walls) — still exists today. It has been built around and over through the centuries, but it has never been torn down and replaced.

Ambrose on Agnes

St. Ambrose could think of no better way to start his treatise on virginity than by referring to St. Agnes, who by his time was already a famous example of holy virginity, second only to the Blessed Virgin Mary. To set the mood for his discussion, he tells her story — a story of courage and heroism as exhibited by a saint who was barely more than a little girl.

Incidentally, when Ambrose says that today is Agnes' "birthday," he means the day of her martyrdom. The early Christians counted a saint's death as the beginning of her real life and celebrated it as her "birthday."

It's a good time to start this work. Today is the birthday of a virgin, and I have to speak of virgins. Here's the beginning for my book!

This is the birthday of a martyr: let us offer the victim. It's the birthday of St. Agnes: let men admire, let children take courage, let the married be astonished, let the unmarried take her for an example.

But what can I say about someone whose name itself shone with praise? She was beyond her age in devotion, above nature in her virtue. It seems to me that she bore not so much a human name as a sign of martyrdom, by which she showed what she was going to be. [The name Agnes comes from a Greek word meaning "holy" or "chaste"; in Latin, it means a young lamb.]

But I do have something that will help. The name "virgin" is a title of modesty. I will call on the martyr. I will proclaim the virgin. Any praise is long enough if it doesn't need to be explained but is already within our grasp.

So let labor cease. Let eloquence be silent. One word is praise enough — the word that old and young alike chant. No one is more worthy of praise than one who can be praised by all. There are as many heralds as there are human beings, proclaiming the martyr when they speak.

They say that she suffered martyrdom when she was twelve years old. What hateful cruelty, not even sparing such a tender age! But truly so much the greater was the power of faith that showed itself even in that age. Was there even room for a wound in that little body? Yet she who had no room for the blow of the steel had what it took to overcome the steel. Normally, girls of that age can't even bear angry looks from their parents, and they cry at pinpricks as though they were wounds. She was fearless under the cruel hands of the executioners, unmoved by the weight of the creaking chains. She offered her whole body to the sword of the raging soldier. She was still ignorant of death, but she was ready for it. If she had been unwillingly hurried to the altars, she was ready to stretch out her hands to Christ at the sacrificial fires, and to make the sign of the Lord, the Conqueror, at the sacrilegious altars themselves. She was ready to place her neck and both her hands in the iron bands — but no bands could hold such slender limbs!

Here's a new kind of martyrdom. Not old enough to be punished yet, but already ripe for victory — hard to contend with but easy to be crowned — she took on the job of teaching valor in spite of her youth. If she had been a bride, she would not have hurried to the couch as quickly as, still a virgin, she joyfully went to the place of punishment with a quickened step. Her head was adorned, not with braids, but with Christ. Everyone wept; she alone was without a tear. Everyone wondered that she was so careless of her life, which she had not yet enjoyed, but was giving up now as though she had used it up. Everyone was astonished that she was ready to bear witness to God, though she was too young to make her own decisions. And though her evidence about a man would not have been accepted, she managed to make herself believed about God.

Whatever is beyond nature is from the Author of nature.

What threats the executioner used to make her fear him! What attractions he used to persuade her! How many wished she would marry them!

But she answered, "It would be an insult to my Spouse to think that anyone was likely to please me. He chose me first for himself; he will have me. Executioner! Why do you delay? Let this body perish, if it can be loved by eyes I don't want to love it."

She stood; she prayed; she bent down her neck. You could see the executioner tremble, as though he had been condemned himself. His right hand shook. His face grew pale. He feared the peril of another, while the girl didn't fear her own.

Here, then, you have two martyrdoms in one victim: a martyrdom of modesty and a martyrdom of religion. She remained a virgin, and she gained martyrdom.[6]

— *NPNF2* 10:364

What Is Juno to Agnes?

Like many Christian thinkers, St. Augustine believes that the pagan "gods" were originally mortals who had received divine honors. After all, emperors like Nero and Claudius were counted among the gods, and everyone knew how they got there — by proclamation of the Roman Senate.

So how much are these "gods" worth? Not as much as the weakest faithful Christian, says Augustine. A sick old man is more powerful than Hercules. And a thirteen-year-old girl, Agnes, conquered the devil — the source of all these delusions about "gods" and "goddesses."

Happy the martyrs whose acts we have read! Happy that St. Agnes who suffered on this same day! A pious virgin, well did she bear her name. In Latin, "Agnes" means a young lamb; in Greek, the word means "chaste." She was all this; she was righteous as she was crowned.

Now, my friends, what shall I say about those men to whom pagans gave divine honors — to whom they consecrated temples, priests, altars, and sacrifices? What shall I say? You can't compare them to our martyrs! Nothing I can say is sufficient for the martyrs. No matter how feeble the faithful are while they are still in the flesh, even if they can't eat food but only milk, far be it from our thoughts to compare them to these sacrilegious gods!

Measured against a poor old but faithful Christian woman, what is this Juno? What is this Hercules measured against an old Christian man, sick and trembling in every limb? This famous Hercules triumphed over Cacus, and a lion, and Cerbreus. Fruitful [the martyr] triumphed over the whole world! Though she was only thirteen years old, Agnes triumphed over the devil. Yes, that child conquered the very devil who had duped so many on the subject of Hercules.

— St. Augustine, Sermon 273, from *Oeuvres complètes de Saint Augustin, Traduites pour la première fois, sous la direction de M. Raulx*, Bar-le-Duc, 1869.

Prudentius: The Tale of St. Agnes

This is the story of St. Agnes the way the Romans loved to tell it. Prudentius, one of the best Christian poets of the age, is a great storyteller, and the tale of St. Agnes gives him a subject worthy of his talent.

In Prudentius, we see what baffled and horrified educated pagans about the Christians: here's a Christian poet choosing a little girl for his epic hero! What had happened to literary standards? Did Agnes ever kill a bunch of Trojans? Did she ever disembowel anybody at all? What kind of hero is it that just bows her head and lets a common soldier chop it off?

But the pagans were rapidly losing that battle. Agnes and martyrs like her were the heroes ordinary Romans wanted to hear about. And Prudentius gave them the perfect Christian entertainment: a story that not only thrilled them while they heard it but left them longing to imitate the Christian virtues of Agnes.

> In Romulus' old home is Agnes' tomb,
> The tomb of a brave girl, a famous martyr.
> Within the very sight of Roman towers,
> The virgin guards the safety of the Quirites.[7]
> Nor does she fail in watching over pilgrims
> Praying to her with pure and faithful hearts.
>
> The martyr wears a brilliant double crown:
> Virginity untouched by any crime
> And then the glory of the death she chose.
>
> They say that, still not ready to be yoked
> In marriage — nothing but a little girl —
> She burned for Christ, and steadfastly refused
> The impious demand to turn away
> From holy faith and sacrifice to idols.
> Allured at first by many kinds of tricks —

Now by the tempting mildness of the judge,
Now by the raging fury of the butcher —
She stood with fierce and pertinacious strength,
And offered up her body to the torturer
For torment, not refusing even death.

Then said the angry tyrant, "If she thinks
It's not so hard to bear the simple pain
We've brought against her, and she sets her life
At nothing, the virginity to which
She's consecrated is another thing.
She shall be thrown into a public brothel
Unless she bows her head before the altar
At once, and begs the pardon of Minerva,
The virgin whom this virgin has disdained
So hastily. And all the boys will run
Into the place to seek their newest toy."

"No, no," said Agnes. "Christ will not forget
His own, so that our golden modesty
Should thus be lost. He will not fail us now.
He helps the modest, and will not allow
A stain upon his sacred gift of purity.
Dye your sword in my blood, sir, if you like;
My body will not be defiled by lust."

And thus she spoke. The judge then sent the virgin
To be exposed in public in the square.
The melancholy throngs all faded back,
Their eyes averted: no one dared to fix

His gaze on her with bold impertinence.
But one, by chance, did boldly turn his face
Toward the girl, and did not fear to look
Upon her holy form with lustful eye.
Behold! A flame of burning fire shot
Like lightning down to strike him in the eyes!
He fell down blinded by the flash of light
And lay there quivering in the dusty street.
His friends retrieved him, now half-dead, and mourned
His fate with piteous words of lamentation.
The virgin went out praising God the Father
And Christ in holy and triumphant song,
That, when in danger of a dreadful stain,
Virginity had conquered, and had found
The very brothel to be pure and spotless.
Some say that Agnes, asked to pray to Christ
That he restore the vanished light, poured out
Her prayers, so that the blinded youth was healed:
His eyes renewed, the breath of life returned.

But Agnes now had taken her first step
Into the vestibule of heaven. Soon
Another would be given her to climb.
Fury stirred up the bloody enemy:
He sighed with rage and said, "She's beaten me!
Go, soldier, draw your sword, and execute
The royal orders of the highest prince!"

When Agnes saw the savage standing there
With his blade drawn, with greater joy she said,

"It's more delight to me to see a soldier,
Mad, savage, and disordered, than a lover,
A soft and languid perfumed boy who comes
To tempt me to destroy my chastity.
No, I say, here's the lover I prefer!
And I will go to meet him when he comes,
Nor will I turn away from his advances.
I'll take the iron deep into my breast,
and draw it all the way into my heart.
Thus as the bride of Christ I'll leap above
The shadows of the world into the light.
Eternal Ruler! Open up the gates
Of heaven, which before were closed to mortals,
And call my soul, with my virginity,
To follow you, a sacrifice to God."

So saying, Agnes bowed her head in prayer
To Christ, her neck bent for the coming wound.

Thus, by the soldier's hand, her hope came true:
A single blow struck off her head, and death
Came over her before she felt the pain.

Her spirit, now set free, flies up to heaven
Along a path of light among the angels.
She marvels at the world beneath her feet,
And, up on high, she views the shades below
And laughs to see the sun turn in its circle;
The world that turns around it and surrounds it;
The dark tornado of the life we live;

The vanity of our inconstant age,
With kings and despots, power, wealth, and rank,
The pomp of honor and of stupid pride,
The furious thirst for silver and for gold
Grasped at by all with countless infamies;
The palaces built up with so much splendor;
The vanity of rich embroidered robes;
The anger, fear, and longing, and the dangers —
Now a long sadness, now a fleeting joy —
The burning fires of dark malicious envy
That blacken every human hope and honor;
And, what is vilest out of all these evils,
The grubby clouds of pagan ignorance.

These things beneath her feet the virgin crushes,
And with her heel she breaks the dragon's head:
That savage beast that poisons everything
Upon the earth is plunged into the pit.
Completely conquered by the maid, he lies,
His fiery head pressed down, and dares not rise.

Meanwhile the martyr's spotless brow is crowned
With double crown: one sixtyfold reward,
With tenfold peaks shines with eternal light;
The other, harvest of a hundredfold.

O happy virgin! O unheard-of glory!
O noble dweller in the heavenly mansions!
Listen to us here in our misery,
You who are crowned with double diadem;

To you alone the Father of all has given
Power to purify a public brothel!
I will be purged by the radiance of your prayers
If only you will deign to fill me up.
Nothing is shameful where you gaze upon it,
Or where your holy foot will deign to tread.

— Prudentius, *Peristephanon*, Hymn 14, new translation

Ambrose: Hymn to St. Agnes

This hymn to St. Agnes seems to have been popular immediately, and its reputation has never wavered. Countless poets have translated it into countless languages. Our translation tries to stick as close as possible to the literal meaning of Ambrose's words, while preserving something like his meter.

For Agnes, blessed virgin girl,
This is the day of festival,
When, sanctified by her own blood,
She gave her spirit up to heaven.

She was of age for martyrdom,
Though not of age for marrying —
Yet anyone would think she came
To wed, so happy does she look.

To altars of a devilish god
She's led to burn an offering:
But she responds, "No, never will

Christ's virgins hold a torch like that.

"This is the fire that snuffs out faith;
This is the flame that steals our light.
Here — strike me here — and let my blood
Spring forth at once to douse the fire!"

They strike her — but what dignity!
She pulls her robe to cover her
And seeks the ground on bended knee,
And, in all modesty, falls down.

Jesus, to you be glory given,
To you, who were of Virgin born;
And to the Father and the Spirit,
Throughout the everlasting ages.

—St. Ambrose, *Hymn to St. Agnes*, new translation

Chapter 4

Poets and Thinkers

There were a few pagan women who earned fame as poets or philosophers, but they were very few. We can't say that women were commonly poets and philosophers among the Christians either, but the number seems to have been significantly higher. What's especially remarkable is the way the men around them took these great thinkers of the early Church seriously — and often deferred to their opinions. St. Gregory of Nyssa, for example — himself one of the greatest theologians in history — always referred to his sister Macrina as "the Teacher," because he believed that he had learned much of what was valuable in his own thought from her. He wrote down his conversations with her in a series of dialogues, and he also wrote a biography of her in which he praises her wisdom and knowledge as much as her saintly life.

ST. MACRINA

Macrina (c. 330-c. 379) came from a truly extraordinary family. Her brothers, St. Gregory of Nyssa and St. Basil the Great, are two of the most important Fathers of the Church. Yet Gregory was always ready to grant her the intellectual superiority in their discussions: in the conversations with her that he wrote down, Gregory is the one who gets things wrong or gives in to despair, and Macrina is the one who sets him right.

Gregory remembered his sister as a great thinker above all. She lived a holy and exemplary life, and she had great strength of character. But it was her mind that really stood out. She was capable of rigorous argument and subtle distinctions, often clearing up puzzles that baffled her brother. But she always based her reasoning on sound faith and unshakable charity. Her thoughts were valuable precisely because they were not idle speculations but instead carefully reasoned arguments from the known truths of Christian doctrine.

The Education of Macrina

In his biography of his sister, Gregory tells us that her qualities of mind showed themselves at a very early age. A strong and determined mother saw to it that Macrina didn't get her ideas about life from the popular entertainment that usually made up a girl's education. Instead, she studied Scripture, and the results proved that a proper education was at least as likely to produce a fine mind in a girl as in a boy.

Her mother was responsible for the child's education. But she did not make use of the usual worldly method of education, which makes a habit of using poetry as a teaching aid in the early years of the child. She considered it disgraceful and very inappropriate that a tender and impressionable nature should be taught either those tragic passions of womanhood that give the poets their ideas and their plots, or the indecencies of comedy, defiling her, so to speak, with unseemly stories of women's intrigues.

The parts of Scripture that you would think young children could never understand were the subject of her studies — in particular the Wisdom of Solomon, and especially the parts of it that have to do with ethics. And there was no part of the Psalms that she did not know. She recited every part of it at set times. When she got out of bed, or did her chores, or rested, or ate food, or left the table, or went to bed, or rose to pray in the middle of the night, the Psalms were her constant companion, like a good fellow traveler that never deserted her.

So she filled her time with these occupations and others like them, and besides that she gained some considerable skill in wool work. Thus, the growing girl reached her twelfth year, when the bloom of adolescence begins to appear. It's worth mentioning that the girl's beauty could not be concealed, no matter how hard she tried to hide it. It seems that, compared with all the others, there was nothing as wonderful as her beauty in the whole countryside. She was so lovely that even painters could not do justice to her: the art that depicts everything and dares the greatest tasks, even imitating the forms of the heavenly bodies, could not reproduce the loveliness of her form accurately.

Naturally, swarms of suitors crowded around her parents, seeking her hand in marriage. Her father, though, was a clever man, known for making the right decisions. Out of all those suitors, he picked out a young man who was just leaving school. He was related to the family, of good birth and remarkably reliable. To this young man he decided to betroth his daughter as soon as she was old enough. Meanwhile, there was great hope for the young man: he offered to his future father-in-law his fame in public speaking, like a bridegroom's gift — for he showed the power of his eloquence in debates on behalf of those who had been wronged.

But envy cut off these bright hopes and snatched the poor boy away from life.

Now, Macrina was not ignorant of her father's plans. But when the arrangement that had been made for her was shattered by the death of the young man, she said that her father's intention was equivalent to a marriage, and she resolved to stay single from then on, just as if the intention had actually been carried through.

And her determination was certainly more solid than could have been expected from someone her age. When her parents brought her proposals of marriage — which often happened, with all the suitors attracted by the fame of her beauty — she would say that it was absurd and unlawful not to be faithful to the marriage that had been arranged for her by her father, but to be compelled to consider another. In the nature of things there is only one marriage, she said, as there is only one birth and one death. She insisted that the man whom her parents' arrangement had tied to her was not dead: since he lived in God, thanks to the hope of the resurrection, he was only absent, and it was wrong not to keep faith with the bridegroom who was away.

These were the arguments she used to turn away those who tried to talk her out of her decision. And she decided on a way of sticking to her good resolution: she resolved not to be separated from her mother, even for a moment. Her mother often said that she had carried the rest of her children in her womb for the usual time, but she was still bearing Macrina, since in a sense she always carried her around with her.

But the daughter's companionship was not a burden to her mother; in fact, it was useful. Her daughter paid as much attention to her as many maidservants, and the benefits were mutual. The mother looked after the girl's soul, and the girl looked after her mother's body and did everything she needed for her, even down to cooking the meals with her own hands. Not that she made that her main business, but after she had anointed her hands by doing her religious duties (since she thought that zeal for those duties was consistent with the principles of her life), she made food for her mother by her own toil.

Not only that, but she helped her mother out with her other responsibilities. Her mother had four sons and five daughters, and she paid taxes to three different governors, since her property was in three different districts. Her father had passed away by this time, so her mother was distracted with all her anxieties. In all these things, she shared her mother's labor, dividing the worry with her, and lightening her heavy burden of sorrows. At the same time, with her mother as guardian, she was keeping her own life blameless, so that her mother's eye both directed and witnessed everything she did. And by her own life, she gave her mother considerable instruction, leading her to the same goal (I mean philosophy) and gradually drawing her on to the immaterial and more perfect life.

— St. Gregory of Nyssa, *Life of St. Macrina*,
online at tertullian.org/fathers

A Teacher to the End

Even as she lay dying, Macrina was teaching. Her brother Gregory was inclined to give in to despair: their brother Basil had already died, and now he was losing his sister as well. Macrina saw that her brother was floundering, and she pulled herself together and gave him the encouragement he needed.

A man led me to the house where my great sister was, and he opened the door. Then I entered that holy dwelling.

I found her already terribly weak. She was lying on the floor, not on a bed or couch. A sack had been spread out on a board, and another board propped up her head, arranged like a pillow, slanting to support her neck muscles and holding up her neck comfortably.

When she saw me at the door, she raised herself up on her elbow. Her strength was already drained by the fever, so she could not come to meet me; but she showed the respect due my rank[8] by putting her hands on the floor and leaning over from her pallet as far as she could.

I ran over to her and embraced her as she lay there. Then I lifted her up and put her back in her usual position.

Then she lifted up her hand to God and said, "You have also granted me this favor, O God, and you have not deprived me of my desire, because you have induced your servant to visit your handmaid."

She didn't want to make me unhappy, so she stifled her groans and did her best to hide the trouble she had breathing. She tried to be cheerful in every way: she took the lead in friendly talk herself, and she asked questions to give us an opportunity to respond.

In the course of conversation, someone mentioned the great Basil, and my face fell into gloom. But she was so far from sharing my grief that she treated the mention of the holy one as an occasion for even loftier philosophy: she discussed all sorts of subjects, looking into human affairs and revealing as she talked the divine purpose hidden in disasters. Besides that, she discussed the future life as if she were inspired by the Holy Spirit. I almost felt as though, with the help of her words, my soul was lifted up out of this mortal nature and placed in the temple of heaven.

We learn in the story of Job that the saint was tormented in every part of his body with discharges from the infection of his wounds, but he did not allow the pain to affect his reason. In spite of the pain in his body, he did not slack off on his activities or interrupt the lofty flow of his conversation.

I saw the same thing in this great woman. Fever was drying up her strength and driving her on to death, but she refreshed her body with dew, as it were, and kept her mind unobstructed in contemplating heavenly things, not a bit injured by her weakness. And if I hadn't already carried on my story to an inexcusable length, I'd tell you everything as it happened — how she was uplifted as she talked with us on the nature of the soul and explained the reason of life in the flesh, and why we were made, and how we were mortal, and the origin of death, and the nature of the journey from death to life again. In all that, she told her tale clearly and in order, as if she had been inspired by the power of the Holy Spirit. And the even flow of her language was like a fountain, with water continuously streaming down.

— St. Gregory of Nyssa, *Life of St. Macrina,*
online at tertullian.org/fathers

Macrina Against the Atheists

As he talked with his dying sister, Gregory let all his doubts come out. How do we even know there is a God? What can we say to an atheist? Macrina attacks the problem head-on, showing that she had absorbed the best scientific thought of the day as well as the principles of Christian doctrine. Her argument is one that theologians still make today: the way the world fits perfectly together proves that a divine mind is at work.

I said, "That's exactly where our adversaries can't fail to have doubts: when we say that all things depend on God and are encompassed by him, or that there is any divinity at all that transcends the physical world."

"It would be better," she cried, "to be silent about such doubts, and not deign to make any answer to foolish and wicked ideas like those. For there is a divine precept that forbids us to answer a fool in his folly, and whoever says there is no God must be a fool, as the prophet declares [see Psalm 14:1].

"But since I have to speak, I'll give you an argument that doesn't come from me, or from any human being — for it wouldn't be worth much if it did, no matter who spoke it. This is an argument that the whole creation speaks through its wonders to the eye as its audience, with a skillful and artistic speech that reaches the heart.

"The creation proclaims the Creator outright. The very heavens, as the prophet says, are telling the glory of God [see Psalm 19:1] with their unutterable words. We see the universal harmony in the wonderful sky, and on the wonderful earth: how elements essentially opposed to each other are all woven together in an indescribable union to serve one common purpose, each contributing its particular force to maintain the whole. We see how things that don't mix, that are mutually repellent, don't fly apart from each other because of their individual properties, and the contrary properties don't destroy them when they're put together. We see how elements that are naturally buoyant move downward — as the heat of the sun, for example, descends in its rays — while heavy bodies are lifted up by being vaporized, so that water ascends, against its nature, and is conveyed by the air to the upper regions. We see, too, how the fire of the firmament penetrates the earth, so that even its deepest chasms feel the heat. We see how the moisture of the rain soaks into the soil and generates countless different seeds, even though it is one by nature, and animates each thing under its influence in due proportion. We see how fast the polar sphere turns, and how the orbits within it move in the opposite direction, with all the eclipses and conjunctions and measured intervals of the planets.

"We see all this with the piercing eyes of the mind, and we can't fail to learn from such a spectacle that a divine power, working with skill and method, is showing itself in this world right now. It penetrates every part, combines the parts with the whole, and completes the whole with the parts. It encompasses the universe with a single all-controlling force, self-centered and self-contained, never ceasing from its motion, yet never changing its position."

— *NPNF2 5:432-433*

PROBA THE POET

Proba (c. 306-c. 353) was a Christian noblewoman who had obviously had a thorough education in literature and the classics. Only someone who had practically memorized Virgil would undertake to compose a Virgilian cento, as she did.

A *cento* is a poem made up of lines from other poems. The word means a patchwork, like the thick patchwork cloaks Roman soldiers used as quilted armor. The rules of the cento are very strict and mind-bogglingly difficult. Every line or half-line must be taken from a famous poet; it's possible to take lines in the same cento from more than one poet, but Proba deliberately chose to limit herself to Virgil. Nothing shorter than about half a line is allowed, but on the other hand no two lines can be taken together. Proba allowed herself to change proper names to the names of biblical characters, as long as they fitted the meter.

The cento was actually a common form of literature in Proba's time. Her work required extreme cleverness and an encyclopedic knowledge of Virgil. Try to make a new biography of George Washington using only lines from Milton's *Paradise Lost* and you'll have a rough idea of the task Proba was taking on. For the poet, the pleasure was something like solving a very hard puzzle; for the reader, the pleasure was in recognizing the lines of Virgil even as they told a completely new story. For Proba in particular, there must have been an added pleasure in turning Rome's greatest poet into a Christian.

Certainly using Virgil to tell the story of Christ was a daring enterprise. It was sure to offend a lot of people on both sides. The remaining pagans, of whom there were many, would be offended at seeing the closest thing Rome had to a canonical scripture being perverted to Christian ends. And many Christians were deeply suspicious of all pagan literature; more than a few condemned Proba's taking over a pagan poet's words as wholly inappropriate for a Christian. St. Jerome condemned Christianized Virgil in general, and he probably had this particular poem in mind when he said, with his usual gift for colorful insults, that "all this is childish, and resembles the sleight-of-hand of a mountebank."

On the other hand, many Christian writers approved of Proba's work, and the mere fact that we still have it shows that it was much loved in certain circles. Even the fact that Jerome panned it shows that he knew of it and had read it.

The elliptical and allusive language of the poem would tax the patience of most modern readers. A fair sample is this passage, in which Proba tells us of the time

... When first the woman who wore a virgin's face
And garment bore — O marvelous to tell! —
A son who was not of our race or blood,
And awful prophets sang their oracles:
That there should come a man to lord it over
Peoples and lands, whose seed comes down from
        heaven;
Who with his courage would subdue the world,
His empire ending only at the ocean,
His fame unbound but by the stars themselves.

— Proba, *Cento*, new translation

This is a description of the Incarnation. Proba's cleverness in adapting Virgil to the story of the Gospel was the thing that her contemporaries most admired. But it was also a deliberate act of subversion: Virgil was the last arbiter of correctness in the Latin language, and thus the basis of an education in grammar. To turn Virgil's words into the Gospel story was a slap at the pagans, but it was also a suggestion of a different way of thinking about the literary heritage of the Latin language. Instead of rejecting everything written by a pagan, Christians could admire and preserve what was good in Roman literature. And it's certainly true that almost everything we have of ancient pagan literature is preserved because Christians in the Middle Ages took the trouble to preserve it.

ST. MARCELLA, ST. PAULA, AND ST. EUSTOCHIUM

Marcella (d. 410) herself was one of Jerome's close friends. Eighteen letters of his to her have been preserved, in addition to the following one from Paula and Eustochium.

The thing that stood out about Marcella was her insatiable intellectual curiosity. She had faith, but she wanted knowledge — and she wanted it from the most reliable source. Jerome was certainly on anybody's short list of smartest men in the world at that time, so she went to him, repeatedly, with the most difficult questions she could think up. And she didn't just accept the first explanation that popped into his head either. She argued with him. He might have been the greatest biblical scholar of his age, but she could send him scurrying back to his books to find a better explanation. Jerome sometimes called her a slave driver, and he complained once that she had kept him up all night until he got a stomachache doing research to satisfy her demands.[9] But the notoriously crusty Jerome wouldn't do that sort of thing for just anybody. He did it for Marcella because she was asking real questions that really were hard to answer, and he knew that she had the intellectual equipment to understand the answer once he found it.

Marcella was the first of the noble Roman ladies to embrace a monastic life, or at least the first to admit it in public ("it seemed so strange and disgraceful and degrading then," Jerome remembered). She turned her house into not just a community of Christian women but also a kind of academy where women could study Scripture and theology under some of the best minds in the business — not least of whom was Marcella herself. She taught many men too: Roman priests came to know that, if you had a tricky question about Scripture, Marcella was the one to ask — although she was always careful to attribute her teaching to some famous man in the Church, to avoid offending delicate male sensibilities.

Paula (347-404) and Eustochium (c. 368-c. 419) were a mother and daughter from a noble Roman family who learned the faith in Marcella's school. Some time later they moved to Palestine to take up a religious life. Both had extraordinarily sharp and inquiring minds, and they sought out Jerome to give them a sort of graduate-level course in Scripture and theology. Both were equally fluent in Latin and Greek, and both also learned to read the Old Testament in the original Hebrew. Eustochium, in fact, was such a remarkable woman that Jerome describes her as "that paragon of virgins," and he invites us to judge

Marcella's accomplishments by her having produced such a pupil as Eustochium.

Together, these great women show us what extraordinary intellectual heights Christian women had scaled in Rome of the 300s. Marcella was a pioneer, but by the end of her life it had become quite fashionable for Christian women in Rome to devote their lives to prayer and learning.

Come to Palestine and Meet Everybody

In this letter, Paula and Eustochium plead with Marcella to join them in Palestine. They make a passionate argument for the attractions of the Holy Land as the scene of so much of biblical history, but most importantly as a place where all of the most brilliant minds in the Christian world are gathered. As Athens is the center of pagan learning, they say, so Jerusalem is the Christian Athens. But more than that, it's a place where the most outstanding figures in Christian intellectual life can live in perfect Christian humility and equality. The appeal is at once to Marcella's faith and to her intellectual curiosity.

Jerome may have helped polish up this letter, but it's quite clear that these weren't women who needed help to write down their thoughts. On the contrary, their intellectual attainments would make most of us ashamed of ourselves.

Love can't be measured. Impatience knows no bounds. Eagerness won't stand for delay.

So, forgetting our weakness, and relying more on our will than our capacity, we desire — even though we are pupils — to teach our teacher. We're like the pig in the proverb, which sits down to teach the goddess of invention.

You were the first to light our tinder, the first to urge us — by lesson and by example — to take up the life we live now. As a hen gathers her chicks, you took us under your wing. Now will you let us fly around at random with no mother near us? Will you leave us to dread the swoop of the hawk and the shadow of every passing bird of prey? Separated from you, we do what we can. We make our mournful complaint, and we beg you more by sobs than by tears to give us back the Marcella we love. She is mild, gentle, sweeter than the sweetest honey — she mustn't be stern and surly to us, when her winning ways have stirred us up to take up a life like her own.

If what we ask is for the best, our eagerness to obtain it is nothing to be ashamed of. And if all the Scriptures agree with our view, we are not too nervy when we urge you to do what you yourself have often urged us to do.

What are God's first words to Abraham? "Go from your country and your kindred and your father's house to the land that I will show you" [Genesis 12:1]. The patriarch, first to receive the promise of Christ, is told here to leave the Chaldeans, to leave the city of confusion and its *rehoboth* or broad places [see Genesis 10:11], and to leave the plain of Shinar as well, where the tower of pride had been raised to heaven. He has to pass through the waves of the world and ford its rivers — the rivers next to which the saints sat down and wept when they remembered Zion [see Psalm 137:1], and the torrent of Chebar, from which Ezekiel was carried to Jerusalem by the hair of his head [see Ezekiel 8:3].

Abraham goes through all this so that he may live in a land of promise watered from above, not from below like Egypt [see Deuteronomy 11:10], not a producer of herbs for the weak and sick [see Romans 14:2], but a land that looks for the early and late rain from heaven. It is a land of hills and valleys [see Deuteronomy 11:11] and stands high above the sea. It is entirely lacking in the attractions of the world, but because of that its spiritual attractions are all the greater.

[*From here the letter meanders through biblical history with extraordinary learning. It dwells especially on the history of Jerusalem, which was legendarily the home of Adam, whose skull was said to be buried on Calvary, the very spot where Christ was crucified. All this leads up to the present attractions of Jerusalem for the faithful Christian: not only is it the scene of the great events in salvation history, but it is also the spot where the greatest minds of Christianity have gathered.*]

I don't have time to go through the period that has passed since the ascension of the Lord, or to name the bishops, the martyrs, and the clergymen who have come to Jerusalem because they felt that their devotion and knowledge would be incomplete, and their virtue would lack the finishing touch, unless they adored Christ in the very spot where the Gospel first flashed from the scaffold. A famous orator blames a man for having learned Greek at Lilybaeum instead of Athens, and Latin in Sicily instead of Rome — obviously on the ground that each province has its peculiarities. Can we suppose the education of a Christian is complete without visiting the Christian Athens?

When we say that, we don't mean to deny that the kingdom of God is in the midst of us [see Luke 17:21] or to say that there are no holy men anywhere else. We simply assert in the strongest way possible that those who are foremost throughout the world are gathered here side by side. We ourselves are among the last, not the first, but we have come here to see the first of all nations. Of all the ornaments of the Church, our group of monks and virgins is one of the finest. It's like a fair flower or a priceless jewel.

The Briton, separated from our world, no sooner makes progress in religion than he leaves the setting sun in quest of a spot he has heard of only through Scripture and hearsay. Need we mention the Armenians, the Persians, the Indians, and the Arabians? Or the people from our neighbor Egypt, so rich in monks; from Pontus and Cappadocia, from Lebanon and Mesopotamia and the populous East?

In fulfillment of the Savior's words, "Where the body is, there the eagles will be gathered together" [Luke 17:37], they all gather here and in this city exhibit the most varied virtues. Though they differ in language, they are one in religion, and almost every nation has a choir of its own. Yet among this great throng, there is no arrogance, no disdain of self-restraint. All strive for humility, that greatest of Christian virtues. Whoever is last here is regarded as first. Their dress neither provokes remark nor calls for admiration. However a man appears, he is neither censured nor flattered. Long fasts help no one here. Starvation wins no deference, and taking food in moderation is not condemned. Before his own master each one stands or falls [see Romans 14:4]. No one judges another, lest he be judged [see Matthew 7:1]. Infighting, so common elsewhere, is unknown here. Sensuality and excesses are far removed from us. And there are so many places of prayer in the city that a day would not be enough to visit them all....

Will the time never come when a breathless messenger brings news that our dear Marcella has reached the shores of Palestine, and when every band of monks and every troop of virgins unites in a song of welcome?

In our excitement we are already hurrying to meet you! Without waiting for a carriage, we rush off at once on foot. We'll clasp your hand and gaze on your face. And when at last, after a long wait, we embrace you, we'll find it hard to tear ourselves away.

— *NPNF2* 6:60-65

The Life of Marcella

In writing to Principia, one of Marcella's star students, Jerome can hardly contain his admiration for Marcella's accomplishments. His praise is all the more remarkable because Jerome was well known as a prickly character who was very much aware of the shortcomings of the people around him. In his eyes, one of her chief accomplishments was in helping to guide the Church of Rome through a dangerous period of heresy. According to Jerome, it was Marcella who provided the clear-sighted intellectual leadership the Romans needed when confusion threatened to overwhelm them.

You have often and earnestly begged me, Principia, virgin of Christ, to dedicate a letter to the memory of that holy woman Marcella, and to set forth the goodness we enjoyed so long for others to know and imitate. I am so eager to do her merits justice that I'm sorry you should urge me and imagine that your earnest requests are needed, when not even you can love her more than I do. When I put her outstanding virtues on record, I'll gain more benefit myself than I can possibly give anyone else.

If so far I've kept silent, and allowed two years to go by, it's not because I wanted to ignore her, as you wrongly suppose. It's because of an incredible sorrow: it overcame my mind so much that I decided it was better to keep silent for a while than to praise her virtues in language that wasn't good enough.

Nor will I follow the rules of rhetoric now in eulogizing someone who is so dear to both of us, and to all the saints — Marcella, the glory of her native Rome. I won't bring up her illustrious family and lofty ancestry, nor will I trace her genealogy through a line of consuls and praetorian prefects. I'll praise her for nothing but the virtue that belongs to her — which is all the nobler because, leaving behind both wealth and rank, she sought the true nobility of poverty and humility.

The death of her father left her an orphan, and she had been married less than seven months when her husband was taken from her. Since she was young then, and of noble birth, as well as distinguished by beauty (always an attraction to men) and self-control, a famous man of consular rank, by the name of Cerealis, courted her with great perseverance. Since he was an old man, he offered to make over his fortune to her, so that she might consider herself less his wife than his daughter. Her mother, Albina, went out of her way to win such a protector for her daughter.

But Marcella answered, "If I wanted to marry, instead of dedicating myself to perpetual chastity, I'd look for a husband, not an inheritance."

Her suitor argued that sometimes old men live a long time, while young men die early. She cleverly retorted, "True, a young man may die early, but an old man can't live a long time."

This decided rejection of Cerealis convinced others that they had no hope of winning her hand.

In the Gospel according to Luke, we read this passage:

> And there was a prophetess, Anna, the daughter of Phanuel, of the tribe of Asher; she was of a great age, having lived with her husband seven years from her virginity, and as a widow till she was eighty-four. She did not depart from the temple, worshiping with fasting and prayer night and day. [Luke 2:36-37]

No wonder she earned the vision of the Savior, when she sought him so earnestly. So let's compare her with Marcella — and we'll see that Marcella has the advantage in every way.

Anna lived with her husband seven years. Marcella lived with hers seven months.

Anna merely hoped for Christ. Marcella held him fast.

Anna confessed at his birth. Marcella believed in him crucified.

Anna did not deny the child. Marcella rejoiced in the man as King.

I don't want to make distinctions between holy women on the basis of their merits, as some people have a habit of doing with holy men and leaders of churches. The point I'm making is that both have the same task, and both have the same reward.

Rome used to be a community that loved malicious gossip; it was filled with people from all parts, and it took the prize for wickedness of all kinds. Detraction attacked even the righteous, and worked hard to defile even the pure and clean. In an atmosphere like that, it's hard to escape being smeared. A stainless reputation is hard to get — no, it's impossible. The prophet yearns for it, but hardly hopes to win it: "Blessed," he says, "are those whose way is blameless, who walk in the law of the LORD!" [Psalm 119:1]. Those whose way is blameless are those whose fair fame no breath of scandal has ever sullied, and who have earned no blame from their neighbors. This is what makes the Savior say in the Gospel, "Make friends quickly with your accuser, while you are going with him to court" [Matthew 5:25].

Who ever heard a slander on Marcella that deserved any belief at all? Or who ever believed one without being guilty of malice and defamation? No, she put the Gentiles to confusion by showing them the nature of Christian womanhood, which her conscience and her bearing both showed. Women of the world like to paint their faces with rouge and powder, to wear robes of shining silk, to decorate themselves with jewels, to put gold chains around their necks, to pierce their ears and hang the costliest pearls of the Red Sea in them, and to perfume themselves with musk. While they mourn the husbands they have lost, they rejoice at their escape, and the freedom to choose fresh partners — not, as God wills, to obey them, but to rule over them. For this purpose they choose as their partners poor men who, contented with the mere name of husbands, are more willing to put up with rivals, since they know that they'll be tossed aside at once if they so much as mumble.

But our widow's clothing was meant to keep out the cold, not to show her figure. She wouldn't even wear a gold seal ring, choosing to store her money in the stomachs of the poor rather than to keep it for herself. She never went anywhere without her mother, and she would never without witnesses see the monks and clergy that the needs of such a large house required her to meet with. Her retinue was always made up of virgins and widows — serious and sober ones — since, as she knew very well, the levity of the maids speaks ill of the mistress, and a woman's character is shown by the companions she chooses.

It was unbelievable how much she delighted in the divine Scriptures. She was always singing, "I have laid up your word in my heart, that I might not sin against you" [Psalm 119:11], as well as the words that describe the perfect man, "his delight is in the law of the LORD, and on his law he meditates day and night" [Psalm 1:2]. She understood this meditation on the law, not as a review of the written words (as the Pharisees among the Jews think) but as action, as the apostle said: "So, whether you eat or drink, or whatever you do, do all to the glory of God" [1 Corinthians 10:31]. She also remembered the prophet's words, "Through your precepts I get understanding" [Psalm 119:104], and she felt sure that only when she had fulfilled these precepts would she be permitted to understand the Scriptures. In this sense we read elsewhere that "Jesus began to do and teach" [Acts 1:1] — for teaching is put to shame when your conscience rebukes you, and it's no good preaching poverty or teaching almsgiving if you're rolling in the riches of Croesus, and if — in spite of your threadbare cloak — you still have silk robes at home to keep from the moth.

Marcella practiced fasting, but in moderation. She abstained from eating meat, and she knew wine by its scent more than its taste, touching it only for the sake of her stomach and her frequent ailments [see 1 Timothy 5:23]. She seldom appeared in public, and she took care to avoid the houses of great ladies, so that she wouldn't be forced to look at what she had renounced once and for all. She often went to the basilicas of apostles and martyrs to escape from the crowds and give herself to private prayer.

She was so obedient to her mother that for her sake she did things that she disapproved of herself. For example, when her mother, not caring about her own offspring, wanted to transfer all her property from her children and grandchildren, Marcella wanted the money to be given to the poor instead. Yet she could not bring herself to stand in her mother's way. So she made over her jewels and other belongings to people who were already rich, content to throw her money away rather than sadden her mother's heart.

In those days, no Roman noblewoman had made profession of the monastic life or had ventured to call herself a nun in public — it seemed so strange and disgraceful and degrading then. But some priests of Alexandria, and the patriarch Athanasius, and Peter, to escape the persecution of the Arian heretics, had all fled for refuge to Rome as the safest haven where they could find communion. From them Marcella heard of the life of the blessed Anthony (who was still alive then), of the monasteries of the Thebaid founded by Pachomius, and of the discipline laid down for virgins and widows. And she wasn't ashamed to profess a life that she had learned from them was pleasing to Christ. Many years later, her example was followed first by Sophronia and then by others, of whom it may well be said (in the words of Ennius),

> O! that the axe in Pelion's woods
> Had never cut those pine trees down.

My esteemed friend Paula was blessed with Marcella's friendship, and it was in Marcella's cell that Eustochium, that paragon of virgins, was trained step-by-step. So it's easy to see what kind of teacher she was if she found such pupils.

An incredulous reader may perhaps laugh at me for dwelling so long on the praises of mere women. But just remember how holy women followed our Lord and Savior, ministered to him out of their own possessions, and how the three Marys stood before the cross, and especially how Mary Magdalene (called the "tower" because of the earnestness and glow of her faith) was privileged to see the rising Christ first of all, even before the apostles. Then you'll convict yourself of pride before you convict me of foolishness. For we judge of people's virtue, not by their sex, but by their character. We think the people who are worthy of the highest rank are those who have renounced both rank and wealth. This is why Jesus loved John more than the other disciples: John was of noble birth and known to the high priest, yet he had so little fear of the plots of the Jews that he brought Peter into the high priest's court, and he was the only one of the apostles who was brave enough to take his stand before the cross. He was the one who took the Savior's parent to his own home; it was the virgin son who received the virgin mother as a legacy from the Lord.

Marcella then lived the ascetic life for many years, and she found herself old before it occurred to her that she had once been young. She often quoted with approval Plato's saying that philosophy consists in meditating on death — a truth our own apostle endorses when he says that for your salvation "I die every day" [1 Corinthians 15:31]. Indeed, according to the old copies, our Lord himself says, "Whoever does not bear his own cross and come after me, cannot be my disciple" [see Luke 14:27]. Ages before, the Holy Spirit had said by the prophet, "for your sake we are slain all the day long, and accounted as sheep for the slaughter" [Psalm 44:22]. Many generations later, the words were spoken, "Remember the end of your life, and then you will never sin" [Sirach 7:36] — not to mention that lesson from the eloquent satirist: "Live with death in your mind. Time flies: this word of mine is so much taken from it."

Well, then, as I was saying, she passed her days and always lived with the thought that she must die. Even her clothes were the sort that reminded her of the tomb, and she presented herself "as a living sacrifice, holy and acceptable to God" [Romans 12:1].

When the needs of the Church finally brought me to Rome along with the reverend pontiffs Paulinus (who ruled the church of Antioch in Syria) and Epiphanius (who presided over the church of Salamis in Cyprus), I wanted, in my modesty, to avoid the eyes of noble ladies. Yet she pleaded so earnestly, both "in season and out of season" as the apostle says [2 Timothy 4:2], that at last her perseverance overcame my reluctance. Since, in those days, my name was held in some renown as a student of the Scriptures, she never came to see me without asking some question about them. And she wouldn't accept my explanations at once; she would argue with them — not just for the sake of argument, though, but to learn the answers to the objections she thought someone could make to my statements.

I'm afraid to say how much virtue and ability, how much holiness and purity I found in her. I don't want to go beyond the bounds of what people will believe, and I don't want to increase your grief by reminding you of the blessings you've lost. I'll just say this: whatever in me was the fruit of long study, made part of my nature by constant meditation — she tasted it, she learned it, she made it her own. So when I left Rome, when a dispute came up about the testimony of Scripture on any subject, people went to her to settle it.

She was so wise, and she understood so well what the philosophers call τό πρέπον — that is, what is appropriate — in what she did, that when she answered a question, she didn't give the opinion as one of her own but attributed it to me or to some other source, admitting that she had learned what she taught from others. For she knew that the apostle had said, "I permit no woman to teach" [1 Timothy 2:12]. She did not want to appear to be wronging the male sex, many of whom — sometimes including priests — asked her questions about doubtful and obscure points.

I'm told that you immediately took my place with her; you attached yourself to her, and as they say, you never let so much as a hair's breadth come between her and you. You both lived in the same house, and occupied the same room, so that everyone knew for certain that you had found a mother in her, and that she had found a daughter in you. You found a monastic seclusion for yourselves in the suburbs, and you chose the country instead of the city because of its solitude.

For a long time you lived together. And since many ladies shaped their conduct by your examples, I had the joy of seeing Rome transformed into another Jerusalem. Monastic establishments for virgins became numerous, and there were countless numbers of hermits. In fact, there were so many servants of God that monasticism, which used to be a term of reproach, afterward became a term of honor.

Meanwhile, we consoled each other for our separation by words of mutual encouragement, and discharged in the spirit the debt we could not repay in the flesh. We always went to meet each other's letters, tried to outdo each other in attentions, and anticipated each other in courteous inquiries. Not much was lost by separation when it was so effectively bridged by a constant correspondence.

While Marcella was serving the Lord in holy tranquility this way, a tornado of heresy came up in these provinces that threw everything into confusion. It lashed itself into such a great fury, in fact, that it spared neither itself nor anything that was good. And — as if it weren't enough to have disturbed everything here — it introduced a ship freighted with blasphemies into the port of Rome itself.

The dish soon found a cover for itself, and the muddy feet of heretics fouled the clear waters of the faith of Rome [see Ezekiel 34:18]. No wonder that, in the streets and markets, a soothsayer can strike fools on the back, or pick up his club and shatter the teeth of anyone who criticizes him, when such venomous and foul teaching finds dupes in Rome that it can lead astray.

Next came the scandalous version of Origen's book *On First Principles,* and that "fortunate" disciple who would have been fortunate indeed if he had never fallen in with a master like that. After that came the refutation set out by my supporters, which destroyed the case of the Pharisees and threw them into confusion.

This was when the holy Marcella — who had held back for a long time, not wanting to be suspected of acting from party motives — threw herself into the breach. She knew that the faith of Rome, which had once been praised by an apostle [Romans 1:8], was now in danger, and that this new heresy was drawing in, not only priests and monks, but also many of the laity — besides imposing on the bishop, who imagined that others were as straightforward as he was....

But Marcella was the one who originated the condemnation of the heretics. She provided witnesses first taught by them and then carried away by their heretical teaching. She was the one who showed how many they had deceived, and who brought up against them the impious books *On First Principles,* books that were passing from hand to hand after being "improved" by the hand of the scorpion. And finally, she was the one *who* called on the heretics — in letter after letter — to appear in their own defense. Of course they didn't dare to come. They were so conscience stricken that they let the case go against them by default rather than face their accusers and be convicted by them.

This glorious victory originated with Marcella. She was the source and the cause of this great blessing. You, who shared the honor with her, know that what I say is true. You also know that I bring up only a few of the many incidents, not to tire out the reader with dreary repetition. If I said more, the ill-natured might think I was giving vent to my own spite under the pretext of commending a woman's virtues.

And now on to the rest of my story.

The whirlwind passed from the west into the east, and it threatened to shipwreck many a noble craft as it passed....

While these things were happening, a dreadful rumor came from the west. Rome had been besieged, and its citizens had been forced to buy their lives with gold. Then after they were robbed that way, they had been besieged again, so they lost not just their possessions but their lives.

My voice sticks in my throat. I choke with sobs as I dictate. The city that had taken the whole world was taken itself. Worse than that, famine came before the sword, and only a few citizens were left to be taken captive. In their frenzy, the starving people had recourse to hideous food, and tore one another limb from limb to have meat to eat. Even the mother did not spare the infant at her breast. In the night was Moab taken, in the night did her wall fall down [see Isaiah 15:1]:

O God, the heathen have come into your inheritance;
    they have defiled your holy temple;
    they have laid Jerusalem in ruins.

They have given the bodies of your servants
    to the birds of the air for food,
    the flesh of your saints to the beasts of the earth.

They have poured out their blood like water
    round about Jerusalem,
    and there was none to bury them.

— Psalm 79:1-3

What tongue can tell the slaughter of that night?
What eyes can weep the sorrows and affright?
An ancient and imperial city falls:
The streets are fill'd with frequent funerals ...
All parts resound with tumults, plaints, and fears;
And grisly Death in sundry shapes appears.

— Virgil, *Aeneid,* book 2, translated by Dryden

Meanwhile — as was natural in a scene of such confusion — one of the bloodstained victors found his way into Marcella's house. Now it's my job to tell what I have heard, to relate what holy men have seen — for there were some holy men present, and they say that you were also with her in the hour of danger.

When the soldiers entered, they say, she received them without any look of alarm, and when they asked her for gold, she pointed to her cheap dress to show them she had no buried treasure. They would not believe in her self-chosen poverty, however, but scourged her and beat her with cudgels. They say she felt no pain but threw herself at their feet and pleaded with tears that you might not be taken from her, or —because of your youth — go through what she, as an old woman, had no reason to fear.

Christ softened their hard hearts, and even among bloodstained swords, natural affection asserted its rights. The barbarians took both you and her to the basilica of the apostle Paul, so that you might find a place of safety there, or — failing that — at least a tomb. At that they say Marcella burst into great joy and thanked God for having kept you unharmed in answer to her prayer. She said that she was also thankful that the taking of the city had found her poor, and not made her poor, that she was now in want of daily bread, that Christ satisfied her needs so that she no longer felt hunger, and that she was now able to say in word and in deed, "Naked I came from my mother's womb, and naked shall I return; the LORD gave, and the LORD has taken away; blessed be the name of the LORD" [Job 1:21].

After a few days, she fell asleep in the Lord, but to the last her powers remained unimpaired. She made you the heir of her poverty — or rather she made the poor her heirs through you. When she closed her eyes, it was in your arms. When she breathed her last breath, your lips received it. You shed tears, but she smiled, knowing that she had led a good life, and hoping for a reward hereafter.

In one short night, I have dictated this letter in honor of you, esteemed Marcella, and of you, my daughter Principia — not to show off my own eloquence but to express my heartfelt gratitude to you both. My one desire has been to please both God and my readers.[10]

— *NPNF2* 6:253-258

ST. MONICA

It might seem odd at first to put Monica (333-387) among the poets and thinkers. She would never have thought of herself as an intellectual. She probably had no more than domestic literacy. She could write a grocery list, maybe, and read the signs in the market. Yet she took part in St. Augustine's conversations on profound philosophical matters. She wasn't pretending. She genuinely made the effort to share his intellectual life. Not only that, but she formed his intellect in profound ways. In the dialogues, he often gives her the last word in a discussion.

Augustine was a difficult son — brilliant, but difficult. His father was not a Christian, and his mother could only do so much to lead him to the faith. Just because he was brilliant, he questioned everything. He fell in with the Manichaeans, heretical semi-Christians who believed that there were two equal principles, good and evil, perpetually struggling for supremacy; the human soul was a bit of the good trapped in the world of evil. And it was useless to argue with Augustine, because he could always out-argue anybody in the room.

So Monica prayed, over and over. It was all she could do — that and be a good Christian. But it was enough. Her son did find his way back to the Church, and when he did he realized that one of the greatest examples of the Christian life had been there in front of his eyes all along. She had the patience to wait for her son's conversion, the persistence to keep praying, and the love to stand by him, even when he had fallen away from the Church.

Monica belongs here, then, not because she was a great intellectual, but because she was a great thinker, a great teacher, and a great mother without ever trying to be an intellectual.

Monica's Drinking Problem

As a young girl, Monica fell into the habit of drinking a little bit of wine — and then, apparently, quite a bit of wine. But as her son tells us, her habit didn't stick with her long. As soon as she saw it for what it was, she swore off wine altogether.

Yet — as she, your handmaid, told me, her son — a love of wine had snuck up on her.

When she was still a sober girl, her parents used to send her to pour out wine from the cask. While she was holding the bottle under the opening, before she poured in the wine, she would wet the tips of her lips with a little of it. She didn't have any desire for more than that. It wasn't from any craving for wine; it was just the overflowing high spirits of her time of life, which bubbles up with playfulness, and whose youthful spirits are usually suppressed by the gravity of elders.

So she added daily littles to that little — for whoever despises small things will fall little by little. She fell into the habit of drinking almost her whole little cup full of wine....

With her father, mother, and guardians absent, you were present, Lord — you who have created, who call, and who work some good for the salvation of our souls by means of those who are set over us.

What did you do, then, my God? How did you heal her? Out of another woman's soul you coaxed a hard and bitter insult, like a surgeon's knife from your secret stash. With one slice, you removed all that stinking decay.

The maid who used to follow her to the cellar happened to be angry with her little mistress. When she was alone with her, she threw this vice in her face with a very bitter insult, calling her a drunkard. Stung by this taunt, she recognized her foulness, and immediately condemned and renounced it.

Just as friends pervert us with their flattery, so enemies often correct us with their taunts. She was angry and wanted to irritate her young mistress, not to cure her. And she did it in secret, either because they happened to be alone when the argument came up or because she didn't want to endanger herself by exposing it so late. But you, Lord, Governor of heavenly and earthly things, who convert the deepest torrents to your purposes, and direct the turbulent current of the ages — you heal one soul with the sickness of another.

— *NPNF1* 1:135-136

St. Monica Worries About Her Son

Monica never stopped mothering her son, even when he was grown up and making a reputation in the world as a rhetorician. She would not be satisfied until he was back in the

arms of the Catholic Church, and she moved heaven and
earth to bring about that reconciliation.

Meanwhile, you granted her another answer, as I recall
(I'm passing over quite a bit here, hurrying on to the things
that urge me more strongly to confess to you, and there's a
lot I don't remember). You granted her another answer, by
one of your priests: a certain bishop who was brought up
in your Church and well versed in your books.

My mother begged him to condescend to have some
talk with me, refute my errors, unteach me evil things
and teach me the good things. He used to do that when
he found people were ready to receive his teaching. But
he refused — and very prudently, as I came to see later.
He answered that I was still unteachable: I was puffed up
with the novelty of that heresy. And she had told him how
I had already confounded various inexperienced people
with my aggravating questions. "Just leave him alone for
a while," he said. "Only pray to God for him. As he reads,
he'll discover by himself what that error is, and how great
its impiety."

And he revealed to her how he himself had been
handed over to the Manichaeans by his misguided mother
when he was only a child, and he had not only read but
even written out almost all their books. Without any argument or proof from anyone, he had come to see how much
that sect was to be shunned — and he had shunned it.

When he had said all this, she still would not be satisfied but even more earnestly begged him to have a talk
with me, shedding plenty of tears. He was a little annoyed
at her insistence, and he exclaimed: "Go your way, and

God bless you. It's not possible that the son of these tears should perish."

As she often mentioned to me when we talked, she accepted that answer as if it were a voice from heaven.

— *NPNF1* 1:67

Augustine Sneaks Away

Augustine pulled a rotten trick on his mother when he went to Rome. She didn't want him to go — he had only just broken with the Manichaean heresy and had not yet come back to the orthodox Church. Though she loved him as only a mother can, she feared for his soul. Augustine thought she was being a nuisance, so he lied to her and sneaked away.

We can hear in his own words how that deception haunted him. His mother was a saint, and he owed her better treatment. But God was busy bringing good out of evil. In Italy, Augustine would meet St. Ambrose, who would finally turn him toward the orthodox faith. Instead of answering Monica's immediate prayer to keep Augustine from leaving, God was giving her what she really wanted: to see him an orthodox Christian before she died.

You knew, God, why I was leaving and going there, but you didn't reveal it, either to me or to my mother. She bitterly mourned my leaving, and went with me as far as the sea. But I fooled her: I pretended I had a friend I couldn't leave until he had a favorable wind to set sail. And I lied to my mother and got away. I lied to a mother like that!

And you've also forgiven me for this. Though I was filled up with disgusting pollution, you saved me from the waters of the sea for the water of your grace, which at last, when I was purified, would dry the fountains of my mother's eyes, from which she watered the ground under her face for me every day.

She refused to go back without me, so it was with difficulty that I persuaded her to stay the night in a place close to our ship where there was an oratory dedicated to St. Cyprian. That night I slipped away, but she wasn't miserly with her prayers and weeping.

And what was she asking of you, Lord, with such an abundance of tears? She was asking you not to let me sail!

But you mysteriously understood what she really wanted. You didn't give her what she was asking for then so that you could make me what she was always asking for.

The wind blew and filled our sails, and the shore passed out of sight. The next day she was there, wild with grief, and filled your ears with complaints and groans. You disregarded them.

Meanwhile, through my longings, you were hurrying me on to the end of every longing. The material part of her love for me was whipped out by the just lash of sorrow. But like all mothers — even more than others, in fact — she loved to have me with her. She didn't know what joy you were preparing for her through my absence. Because she didn't know, she wept and mourned. The inheritance of Eve appeared in her agony: she was seeking what in sorrow she had brought forth.

Yet, after accusing my treachery and cruelty, she went back to praying to you for me. And she went back to her usual place, and I went to Rome.[11]

— *NPNF1* 1:84

One With the Divine

Pagan philosophers and devoted Christians both longed for a union with the divine, the perfect unity the philosopher Plotinus called "the One." They expected to find it by long study and meditation. But in this breathtaking passage from his Confessions, *Augustine tells us how he found that ecstatic experience in the conversation of his mother rather than in all the works of the great pagan and Christian philosophers. Monica lived that unity with God that all the greatest thinkers were so laboriously seeking. The secret seemed to be that she had learned detachment from material things: while she still lived, she was able to leave the world behind and ascend in thought to the perfect life of the saints.*

The day was coming when she would leave this life. (You knew that day; we did not.) It happened — and I believe you arranged it by your secret ways — that she and I were standing alone, leaning by the window. We could see the garden of the house in Ostia where we were staying, resting for the trip away from the crowd after the fatigue of a long journey. We were talking very pleasantly alone, "forgetting what lies behind and straining forward to what lies ahead" [Philippians 3:13]; we were trying to figure out together —

in the presence of the Truth, which you are — what kind of life the eternal life of the saints would be, which "no eye has seen, nor ear heard, nor the heart of man conceived" [1 Corinthians 2:9]. We opened wide the mouth of our heart to the celestial streams of your fountain, the fountain of life — which is with you — so that, sprinkled with it according to our capacity, we might somehow consider such a deep mystery.

Our conversation reached the point where the very highest pleasure of the bodily senses, even in the very brightest material light, seemed not only not worthy of comparison, but not worthy even of mentioning, because of the sweetness of that life of the saints. Lifting ourselves up with a more burning affection toward that life, we gradually passed through all bodily things, and even the heaven itself from which the sun, moon, and stars shine down on earth. We soared even higher by our inner meditation and talking and admiring your works. We came to our own minds and went beyond them. We rose up as high as that region of unfailing plenty where you feed Israel forever with the food of truth, and where life is that Wisdom by whom all these things are made — the things that have been, and the things that are to come. And that Wisdom is not made, but she is as she has been and will always be. Rather, it is not possible for her to *have been* and to be in the *future*, but only to *be,* since to have been and to be in the future are not eternal.

While we were talking that way, and straining after her, we slightly touched her with the whole effort of our heart. We sighed, and left the firstfruits of the spirit bound there.

Then we returned to the sound of our own mouth, where the word that is spoken has both a beginning and an end. And what is like your Word, Lord? He remains in himself, without growing old, and he renews all things [see Wisdom 7:27].

This is what we were saying: Suppose the tumult of the flesh were silenced for someone, and the fantasies of earth, water, and air were silenced. Suppose the poles, too, were silenced. Suppose even the soul were silenced to itself, so that it could go beyond itself by not thinking of itself. Suppose all fancies and imaginary revelations were silenced, and every tongue, and every sign, everything that exists by passing away — since, if anyone could listen, all these things say, "We did not create ourselves but were created by him who lives forever." Suppose, after saying this, they were silenced, having only sensitized our ears to him who created them; and suppose he alone spoke — not through them, but spoke himself, so that we could hear his word, not by tongue of flesh or voice of angel or sound of thunder or the shadow of an analogy, but so that we could hear *him*, whom we love in these things. Without all those things, the two of us strained ourselves and with fleeting thought touched on the eternal Wisdom that remains over all. If we could hold onto that — if other very different visions could be taken away, and this one could ravish us who see it, and absorb us, and envelop us in these inner joys, so that all our lives would be eternally like the one moment of knowledge we were sighing after — wouldn't that be to "enter into the joy of your master"? [Matthew 25:21]. And when will that be? When we all rise again. But not everyone will be changed.

I was saying things like that — if not exactly in that way and in those words, still, you know, Lord, that, on that day when we were talking this way, the world with all its delights became worthless to us, even as we spoke.

Then my mother said, "Son, as for me, I don't have any pleasure in anything in this life anymore. I don't know what I want here anymore, and why I'm here, now that my hopes in the world are satisfied. There was just one reason I wanted to linger a little while in this life, and that was to be able to see you a Catholic Christian before I died. My God has given me far more than that. I see you despising all earthly happiness, and made into his servant. What am I doing here?"

I don't really remember how I answered her. Just five days later, however, or not much more, she was weakened by a fever. One day while she was sick, she went into a faint, and for a short time she was unconscious of visible things. We hurried over to her, but she soon regained her senses. Fixing her eyes on my brother and me as we stood beside her, she asked us, "Where was I?" Then, looking at us intently as we stood there senseless with grief, she said, "You'll bury your mother here."

I was silent and kept from weeping, but my brother said something about wishing she could die in her own country and not abroad, as if that were a happier fate.

When she heard these things, she looked anxious and stopped him with her eye. "Look what he's saying!" she said.

Soon after, she said to us both: "Set this body down anywhere. Don't let the care for it trouble you at all. I only ask this: remember me at the Lord's altar, wherever you are."

And when she had said this, she fell silent, in pain with her increasing illness.

I thought about your gifts, invisible God, the gifts you instill in the hearts of your faithful, from which such marvelous fruits spring. And I rejoiced and gave thanks to you. For I remembered how she had always been burning with anxiety about her burial place. She had prepared the spot next to the body of her husband. Since they had lived very peacefully together, she had wanted to add this to her happiness, and have people say, that after her wandering beyond the sea it had been granted to her that they both should lie in the same grave, as they had been united on earth. So little is the human mind capable of understanding divine things!

I didn't know when this useless thought, through the bounty of your goodness, had begun to disappear from her heart. I was full of joy in admiring what she had revealed to me — though in fact, when she said "What am I doing here?" in our conversation by the window, she didn't seem to want to die in her own country.

Afterward I heard that, while we were in Ostia, she was speaking to some of my friends one day when I was away about the contempt of this life and the blessing of death. They were amazed at the courage you, God, had given her, a woman, and they asked her whether she didn't dread leaving her body at such a distance from her own city.

"Nothing is far for God," she answered. "I don't have to worry that he won't know where to raise me up at the end of the world."

On the ninth day of her sickness, the fifty-sixth year of her age, and the thirty-third year of mine, that religious and devout soul was set free from the body.[12]

Chapter 5

Independent Women

One of the consequences of this revolutionary Christian idea of equality in Christ was a new breed of women who made their own decisions and got things done on their own. We've seen that spirit in the New Testament and in the days of the martyrs, but it really took hold once Christianity became the main religion of the Roman Empire.

When we speak of "independence," we don't mean that these women were loners. Usually, it was quite the opposite: they formed strong communities with other women, and even the powerful Helena sought out other women to pray with. But when it came to making important decisions, they made the decision to follow Christ instead of what their families told them to do.

Often they were the organizers of things that no one else could organize — or that no one else had thought to organize. It was a woman who commanded the first big expedition in biblical archaeology, and another woman who set up the first Christian center of learning for women at Rome.

These women didn't wait for a man to have the same idea, and they didn't just politely suggest to someone that something ought to be done. They did what had to be done, and if that meant taking command of the situation, they were ready to do it. They were active, in charge, and probably a bit fearsome if you stood in their way. But they built up the Church, and the men and women who came after them looked back on them as some of the great figures of ecclesiastical history.

ST. HELENA

Helena (d. c. 330) started life as a stable maid, according to some traditions. She married Constantius Chlorus, a rising star in the Roman military. While he was stationed in Britain, she gave birth to their son Constantine. Later on, she was rudely thrust aside by the demands of politics: it was expedient for Constantius to make an alliance by marriage, and Helena suffered the common fate of inconvenient wives among the Roman nobility. But in spite of the divorce, her son was still devoted to her. When Constantine, having converted to Christianity, came out on top in the latest Roman civil war in the year 312, she suddenly found herself the mother of the emperor of all the Romans. She, too, converted to Christianity, and she took her new faith very seriously, filling her life with acts of charity.

She was nearly eighty years old when she had a dream that she interpreted as a vision from God. It demanded that she go to Jerusalem and find the cross on which Christ had been crucified. Perhaps her long years in the cold after her divorce had taught her to handle things by herself; in any case, she organized an archaeological expedition to Palestine — one of the first real attempts at archaeology on record — and prepared to do some digging.

By 326, when Helena saw it, Jerusalem was nearly unrecognizable: it had been destroyed at the end of the Jewish War in the year 70, and again half a century later at the end of the Bar Kochba revolt. The holy sites had been obliterated, and a temple of Venus stood on the site of Christ's tomb.

Helena had the temple razed, and she supervised the excavation of the site. As for the rest, we'll let Socrates Scholasticus tell us what happened.

The story of Helena became one of the Christians' favorite tales. It wasn't just a story about Helena; it was a story that told what a woman could do. Helena didn't just succeed in her own expedition: she set an example, or we might say that she started a trend. Her very public pilgrimage encouraged countless other women to make similar pilgrimages — not least among them Egeria, whose own travelogue we'll be reading a little later.

The Search for the Cross

Socrates Scholasticus gives us the most complete account of Helena's discovery of the true cross. Although he was writing in the early 400s, about a century after the events, he was more than usually careful in dealing with his sources, and historians today rely on him for a fairly objective assessment of the Church history of his time. Socrates emphasizes the miracle that led to the discovery of the cross — a story we would tend to discount today but one that made perfect sense to Socrates and his readers. He also emphasizes the degree to which she personally supervised everything: the demolition of the pagan temple, the excavation of the site, and the construction of a magnificent new church. Her son the emperor gave encouragement to the construction, but it was Helena's project from start to finish, and Socrates gives her the full credit.

Helena was the emperor's mother; when the emperor made the former village of Drepanum into a city, he named it Helenopolis after her. Led by God in a dream, she went to Jerusalem. Finding that what was once Jerusalem was desolate "as a preserve for autumnal fruits" [Isaiah 1:8], as the prophet says, she carefully searched for the tomb of Christ, from which he rose after he was buried, and after a good deal of trouble she found it.

I'll explain the reason for the trouble in a few words: After the passion of Christ, those who embraced Christianity greatly venerated this tomb. But those who hated Christianity covered the spot with a mound of dirt and built a temple of Venus on it. They set up her image there, not caring for the memory of the place. This went on for a long time, until the emperor's mother heard about it. She had the statue taken down, the dirt taken away, and the ground completely cleared.

In the tomb she found three crosses. One of them was that blessed cross on which Christ had hung; the other two were those on which the two thieves crucified with him had died. With them was also found the sign Pilate had made, on which he had inscribed in different letters that the Christ who was crucified was "the King of the Jews."

It was not clear, however, which of the three was the cross they were looking for, so the emperor's mother was considerably distressed. But the bishop of Jerusalem, Macarius, quickly relieved her of this trouble. He solved the doubt by faith: he looked for a sign from God and found it. And this was the sign: a certain woman of the neighborhood, who had been sick for a long time, was now at the point of death. The bishop arranged to have each of the crosses brought to the dying woman, believing that she would be healed when she touched the precious cross. Nor was he disappointed in his expectation. When she was touched with the two crosses that were not the Lord's, she was still dying. But when the third — the true cross — touched her, she was healed right away and recovered her former strength. This was how the real cross was discovered.

The emperor's mother built a magnificent church over the place of the sepulcher, and she named it New Jerusalem, having built it facing that old and deserved city. There she left part of the cross, enclosed in a silver case, as a memorial for those who might wish to see it. The other part she sent to the emperor. He was persuaded that the city would be perfectly secure when that relic was preserved, so he privately enclosed it in his own statue, which stands on a large porphyry column in the forum called Constantine's in Constantinople. (I've written this from what I've heard, but almost everyone who lives in Constantinople insists that it's true.)

Constantine's mother also found the nails with which Christ's hands had been fastened to the cross, and she sent them as well. Constantine made them into bridle bits and a helmet, which he used in his military expeditions.

The emperor supplied all the materials for building the churches, and he wrote to Macarius the bishop to speed up those buildings.

When the emperor's mother had finished the New Jerusalem, she built another church that was not at all inferior to it over the cave in Bethlehem where Christ was born according to the flesh. Nor did she stop there but built a third on the mount of the Ascension.

She was moved so devoutly in all these things that she would pray in the company of women. She invited the virgins enrolled in the register of the churches to a banquet and brought the dishes to the table, serving them herself. She was also very generous to the churches and to the poor.

And having lived a life of piety, she died when she was about eighty years old. Her remains were brought to New Rome,[13] the capital, and placed in the imperial sepulchers.[14]

— NPNF2 2:21-22

Ambrose on the Finding of the Cross

By the time of St. Ambrose, about half a century later, the story of Helena's expedition to find the true cross had already become something like a legend. Helena was not just a figure of history; she was the pattern of the independent Christian woman, getting things done because her conscience had told her they needed to be done. In one of his sermons, Ambrose imagined what must have been going through her mind as she stood on the site of Golgotha.

Helena came and began to visit the holy places, inspired by the Spirit to look for the wood of the cross. She came to Golgotha and said, "Here is the place of battle — but where is the victory? I look for the standard of salvation, but I cannot find it. Am I in royal authority, when the cross of the Lord is in the dust? Am I decked out in gold, when the cross of Christ is in the ruins? It lies hidden still, and so does the very palm of life eternal! How do I know I am redeemed, if redemption itself is not found?"

— AMBROSE, *De Obitu Theodosii*, 43, NEW TRANSLATION

ST. OLYMPIAS

Olympias (c. 360-408), a wealthy widow, presided over a household of consecrated women in the great city of Constantinople, the capital of the eastern half of the Roman Empire. She was also a "deaconess" in the church there —

a word that had a somewhat different meaning in those days. (It comes from the Greek word for "helper," and a "deaconess" had certain special functions in the Church, including helping women undress for baptism.)

We remember Olympias today, especially because she was a close friend of the great preacher St. John Chrysostom, whose rousing sermons earned him the nickname "Golden-Mouthed" (that's what "Chrysostom" means). Sometimes it seemed as though she was his only friend. John was wildly popular with the poor, but his plain speaking had a way of offending the rich. After one too many pointed sermons against extravagance, the empress had him illegally deprived of his position and thrown out of the city. It was Olympias who, at great cost and danger to herself, supported him in his exile with her own money, and much of what we know about John's exile comes from the letters he wrote back to her.

Olympias on Trial

When John Chrysostom was thrown out of Constantinople, there were riots in the streets. Somehow the great cathedral church burst into flames, and each side — pro-Chrysostom and anti-Chrysostom — accused the other of setting the fire. Some of John's supporters were tortured in an attempt to make them confess. Sozomen, a Church historian, tells us that Olympias was hauled before an anti-Chrysostom judge, accused of being one of the incendiaries. Though the judge intimidated her friends, Olympias used her apparently considerable knowledge of Roman law to turn the tables and force the judge to let her go. The judge tried to win a small victory by at least forcing her to acknowledge the legitimacy of Arsacius, who had been appointed Chrysostom's successor. But Olympias would not even give him that satisfaction.

While all these disasters were going on, Olympias the deaconess showed great fortitude. She was dragged before the tribunal, and the prefect demanded to know why she had set fire to the church.

She replied, "My past life ought to avert all suspicion from me, for I have devoted my large property to restoration of the temples of God."

The prefect told her that he was well acquainted with her past course of life.

"Then you ought to appear in the place of the accuser," she continued, "and let someone else judge us."

Since the accusation against her was completely unproved, and since the prefect found that he had no grounds on which he could justly blame her, he changed to a milder charge, as if he just wanted to give her advice, finding fault with her and the other women because they refused communion with his bishop, although it was possible for them to repent and to change their own circumstances.

They were all afraid and deferred to the advice of the prefect, but Olympias said to him:

> It is not right that, after having been publicly slandered without having had anything proved against me in court, I should be obliged to clear myself of charges totally unconnected with the thing of which I was accused. Let me rather take counsel concerning the original accusation that was brought against me. For even if

you resort to unlawful compulsion, I will not hold communion with those from whom I ought to secede, nor consent to anything that is not lawful to the faithful.

When the prefect found that he could not prevail upon her to hold communion with Arsacius, he dismissed her to consult with her lawyers.

— NPNF2 2:414-415

Olympias, the Tower of Constantinople

While John Chrysostom was languishing in exile, he heard news that his friend Olympias was dangerously ill — near death, in fact. When she recovered, she wrote to him and insisted that it hadn't been all that bad. (Knowing that he had been very ill himself, she probably wanted to spare him any further worry.) But he knew better. In his reply to her, he tells her that her example of Christian courage does more for Constantinople than all the towers, walls, and armies the capital of the empire can muster. We don't have to look for courage in the great deeds or monstrous crimes that fill our history books; we'll find more courage in one faithful woman sitting at home, dealing with her own personal calamities but still putting others first.

And now I am very glad and delighted to hear, not only that you have been released from your illness, but above all that you bear the things that happen to you so bravely, calling them all just an idle tale. And this is an even greater thing, that you have applied this name even to your bodily illness, which is evidence of a robust spirit, rich in the fruit of courage. For this is the real proof of refined philosophy: not only to bear misfortunes bravely but to be actually insensible to them, to overlook them, and with such little exertion to wreathe your brows with the garland prize of patience, neither laboring, nor toiling, neither feeling distress nor causing it to others, but — so to speak — leaping and dancing for joy all the while.

So I am rejoicing and leaping for joy. I am in a flutter of delight. I am insensible to my present loneliness, and the other troubles that surround me, because I am cheered and brightened, and not a little proud, on account of your greatness of soul, and the repeated victories you have won. And I am cheered not only for your own sake, but also for the sake of that large and populous city, where you are like a tower, a haven, and a wall of defense, speaking in the eloquent voice of example. Through your sufferings, you teach persons of either sex to roll up their sleeves readily for these contests, to enter the battle with all courage, and to cheerfully bear the toils such contests involve.

And the wonder is that without thrusting yourself into the forum, or occupying the public centers of the city, but sitting all the while in a small house and confined chamber, you serve and anoint the combatants for the contest. While the sea is thus raging round you, and the billows are rising to a crest, and crags and reefs and rocky ledges and fierce monsters appear on every side, and everything is shrouded in the most profound darkness, you, setting the sails of patience, float on with great serenity, as if it was noonday, with calm weather and a favorable breeze wafting you on. So far from being overwhelmed by this grievous tempest, you are not even sprinkled by the spray.

And no wonder: that's what you can accomplish when you have virtue for a rudder.

Merchants and pilots, and sailors and voyagers, when they see clouds gathering up, or fierce winds rushing down upon them, or the breakers seething with foam, keep their vessels moored inside the harbor. If they happen to be tempest tossed in the open sea, they do their best, and they try by every means to bring their ship to some anchorage, or island, or shore.

But you — although such innumerable winds and fierce waves burst upon you together, and the sea is heaved up from its very depths by the severity of the storm, and some are submerged, others floating dead upon the water, others drifting naked upon planks — you plunge into the middle of this ocean of calamities and call all these things an idle tale! You sail on with a favorable breeze in the midst of the tempest. And naturally so. For pilots, even if they are infinitely wise in that science, nevertheless do not have enough skill to withstand every kind of storm; so they often shrink from doing battle with the waves. But the science you have is superior to every kind of storm: the power of a philosophic soul, which is stronger than ten thousand armies, more powerful than arms, and more secure than towers and bulwarks.

— NPNF1 9:297-298

PROBA THE WIDOW

Proba (c. 400) was a rich widow who had established a community of Christian widows and virgins in her household. That was a common and even fashionable thing for rich women to do in her time, when Rome was under attack and the world seemed to be falling apart. But Proba was exceptionally sincere in her desire to live a life devoted to Christ. For advice, she turned to the greatest mind of her time: St. Augustine, whose letters to her still survive.

Set an Example in Prayer

Proba asked Augustine, who by then was a bishop, to teach her something about praying. Augustine responds that widows have a special responsibility to pray eagerly, because widows are supposed to set the example of prayer for the rest of us. No matter how rich you are, he says, you should remember that the only sure wealth is the treasure you build up in heaven. And finally he asks her to pray for him personally, because he knows how hard it is to be a bishop, and how much he needs the prayers of holy women like Proba.

I remember your request, and I remember my promise. I said that, as soon as I was given time and opportunity by the One we pray to, I would write you something about prayer to God.

Now I feel it's my duty to pay off this debt, and — in the love of Christ — to satisfy your pious wish.

Words can't express how happy your request made me. I saw in it how much you care about this terribly important subject. And what more suitable business could you have in your widowhood than to continue in supplications night and day, as the apostle told us: "She who is a real widow, and is left all alone, has set her hope on God and continues in supplications and prayers night and day" [1 Timothy 5:5]?

It might seem remarkable that care about prayer should occupy your heart and claim the first place in it. After all, as far as the world is concerned, you're noble and wealthy, and the mother of such an illustrious family. Though you're a widow, you're not desolate — except that you wisely understand that, in this world and this life, the soul has no sure portion.

So he who inspired you with this thought is certainly doing what he promised his disciples when they grieved, not for themselves, but for the whole human family, and despaired of the salvation of anyone, after they heard from him that it was easier for a camel to go through the eye of a needle than for a rich man to enter the kingdom of heaven. He gave them a marvelous and merciful reply: "With men this is impossible, but with God all things are possible" [Matthew 19:26]. He who can make even the rich enter the kingdom of heaven therefore inspired you with the devout anxiety that makes you think you need to ask my advice about how to pray.

While he was still on earth, he brought Zacchaeus into the kingdom of heaven, even though he was rich [see

Luke 19:8-10]. After he was glorified in his resurrection and ascension, he made many who were rich despise the present world, and he made them more truly rich when he extinguished their desire for riches by giving them his Holy Spirit.

How could you want to pray to God so much if you didn't trust in him? And how could you trust in him if you were putting your trust in uncertain wealth and neglecting the healthy advice of the apostle? "As for the rich in this world, charge them not to be haughty, nor to set their hopes on uncertain riches but on God who richly furnishes us with everything to enjoy. They are to do good, to be rich in good deeds, liberal and generous, thus laying up for themselves a good foundation for the future, so that they may take hold of the life which is life indeed" [1 Timothy 6:17-19].

If you love this true life, then you need to think of yourself as a pauper in this world, however prosperous your lot may be. That is the true life. Though we love the present life very much, it is not worthy to be called "life," no matter how long and happy it is. But the true life is the true consolation promised by the Lord in the words of Isaiah: "I will give him true consolation, peace upon peace" [Isaiah 57:18-19, Septuagint version]. Without that consolation, though in the midst of every earthly comfort, we find ourselves forlorn rather than comforted.

As for riches and high rank and all the other things that people who don't know true happiness imagine will make them happy, what comfort do they bring? It's better to be independent of those things than to have plenty of them. When we possess them, our fear of losing them gives us more pain than the strength of desire we had when we coveted them. We're not made good by possessing these so-called good things — but if we've already become good, then we make these things really good by using them well.

So true comfort is not to be found in these things, but in those things where we find true life....

Taking all these things into account, and whatever else the Lord leads you to know — things that either haven't occurred to me or would take too much time to say right now — strive to overcome the world in prayer. Pray in hope. Pray in faith. Pray in love. Pray earnestly and patiently. Pray as a widow who belongs to Christ.

For although prayer (as he has taught) is the duty of all his members — of all who believe in him and are united to his body — Scripture especially demands that widows be more diligent in prayer.

Scripture honorably names two women by the name of Anna: one [also known as Hannah], the wife of Elkanah, the mother of the holy Samuel; the other, the widow who recognized the Most Holy One when he was still an infant. The former, though she was still married, prayed with sorrow of mind and a broken heart because she had no sons, and she was given Samuel, and she dedicated him to the Lord, because she vowed to do so when she prayed for him [see 1 Samuel 11]. But it's not easy to find what petition of the Lord's Prayer corresponds to her petition, unless it's the last one, "Deliver us from evil," because it was thought an evil to be married and not have offspring as the fruit of marriage.

But notice what Scripture says about the other Anna, the widow.

She never left the Temple but served God with fasting and prayers night and day [see Luke 2:36-37]. In the same way, as I've already mentioned, the apostle said, "She who is a real widow, and is left all alone, has set her hope on God and continues in supplications and prayers night and day" [1 Timothy 5:5]. When the Lord was urging us to pray always and not to give up, he mentioned a widow who persuaded a judge to listen to her suit by constantly asking him, though he was an unjust and wicked man, and one who neither feared God nor cared for anyone else [see Luke 18:2-8]. So we can see how necessary it is for widows to go beyond others in devoting time to prayer, because from widows are taken the examples that are meant to urge everyone else to be earnest in prayer.

What makes this work specially suitable for widows? It must be their bereaved and forlorn condition. So anyone who understands that in this world he is bereaved and forlorn as long as he is a pilgrim away from his Lord will be careful to commit his widowhood, so to speak, to his God as his shield in constant and eager prayer.

So pray as a widow of Christ, though you do not yet see the One whose aid you implore. And though you are very wealthy, pray as if you were poor. For you do not yet have the riches of the world to come, in which you have no loss to fear. Though you have sons and grandchildren and a large household, still pray (as I said already) as if you were forlorn, for we can't be certain that any temporal blessings will stick around to comfort us even in this present life.

If you seek and delight in the things above, you desire things that are everlasting and certain. And as long as you don't actually have them, you should think of yourself as forlorn, even if all your family are spared to you and you live as you like.

And if you act that way, surely your example will be followed by your very devout daughter-in-law, and by all the other holy widows and virgins who are settled under your care. For the more piously you arrange your house, the more you're bound to keep your prayer up eagerly, not getting into the affairs of the world more than the interests of religion require.

By all means remember to pray earnestly for me. I don't want you to be so respectful of this office I bear, which is full of dangers, that you refrain from giving me the assistance I know I need. The household of Christ prayed for Peter and Paul. I rejoice that you are in his household, and far more than Peter and Paul did, I need the prayers of the brethren. Compete with one another in prayer with a holy rivalry. You are not wrestling with one another but with the devil, who is the common enemy of all the saints. "Prayer is good when accompanied by fasting, almsgiving, and righteousness" [Tobit 12:8]. Let each one do what she can; what one of you can't do by herself, she does through one who can do it, if she loves in another what only her own inability keeps her from doing. So don't let someone who can do less keep back the one who can do more, and don't let the one who can do more push the one who can do less too hard. Your conscience is responsible to God; to one another, owe nothing but mutual love.

May the Lord, who is able to do above what we ask or think, listen to your prayers.[15]

— *NPNF1* 1:459-469

EGERIA THE TOURIST

A strange thing happened when Constantine embraced the Christian religion. Suddenly the Roman Empire was overrun with tourists, and a surprising — perhaps a pagan would say "shocking" — number of them were women. Women from every province wanted to see the holy sites: the sites in Palestine especially but also the tombs and memorials of the martyrs all over the empire. Constantine's own mother, St. Helena, set the pattern and started the trend with her quest for the true cross, and she and Constantine adorned every holy site in the East with a basilica.

We're very lucky to have a travel diary from one of these pilgrims, a woman named Egeria (c. late 300s; also spelled Etheria or Aetheria, and sometimes called Sylvia) who came from the far end of the Roman Empire, probably in what is now northwestern Spain or perhaps southern France. She may or may not have been a nun; she wrote to a group of women she calls "reverend sisters" and "dear ladies."

It's hard for us here in the twenty-first century to imagine what a revolution women like Egeria represented. We see Egeria going from one holy site to another, almost as if she were on a package tour. Often she's with a group of people, but there's no indication that she has some sort of permanent male guardian. She makes decisions on her own, and she endures hardships that most men would think twice about even today. A generation or two before, she would have been a freak or a prodigy.

But in her own time she wasn't really unusual. All the holy sites were used to receiving pilgrims like her. They welcomed these female adventurers and had rooms waiting for them. They taught them and learned from them and sent them away with gifts. We know from archaeology, too, that there was a flourishing trade in souvenirs from the top tourist attractions.

These female pilgrims were in the vanguard of what you might call the Christian women's revolution. They were making their own decisions, doing their own thing, seeing the sights, improving their minds, learning for the sake of learning. These were the practical consequences of St. Paul's scandalous dictum, *In Christ there is neither male nor female.*

Climbing Mount Sinai

Nothing would stop Egeria from seeing Mount Sinai, where the Law was given to Moses. The monks who lived there (their successors are still there today) identified the exact spot where the Law had been given on top of the mountain, and they had built a little chapel there. The climb was steep, too steep for horses or camels: it had to be done on foot. (That's still true.) It took a lot of courage — in fact, it's still an athletic feat today, even for someone in peak condition. But nothing was going to stop a determined woman who had already traveled from the other end of the world.

We reached the mountain late on the sabbath. When we arrived at a certain monastery, the monks who lived there received us very kindly, showing us every kindness. There's also a church and a priest there.

We stayed there that night, and early on the Lord's Day, together with the priest and the monks who lived there, we began to go up the mountains one by one.

It takes infinite toil to go up these mountains. You can't go up a spiral path — the snail-shell way, as we call it — but you climb straight up the whole way. It's like climbing up a wall. And you have to come straight down each mountain until you reach the very foot of the middle one, which is called Sinai proper.

Going this way, at the bidding of Christ our God, and helped by the prayers of the holy men who went with us, we came to the summit of Sinai at the fourth hour. This is the place where the Law was given: that is, the place where the glory of the Lord descended on the day when the mountain smoked. And even though it was so much work — I had to go up on foot, since the ascent is impossible in the saddle — still, it didn't feel like work going up, because I realized that, at God's bidding, I was fulfilling my desire.

There's a church at that place now. It's not very big, since the place itself — the top of the mountain — is not very big. Nevertheless, the church itself is great in grace.

So when, at God's bidding, we had come to the top of the mountain, and had reached the door of the church, the priest who was appointed to the church came from his cell and met us. He was a hearty old man, a monk since early in life, and an "ascetic," as they say here — in short, someone who was worthy to be in that place. The other priests also met us, together with all the monks who lived on the mountain; that is, the ones who were not held back by age or ill health. But no one lives at the very peak of the central mountain. Nothing is there but the church and the cave where holy Moses was.

The whole passage from the book of Moses was read in that place, and the sacrifice of the Mass was properly celebrated. Then, as we were coming out of the church, the priests of the place gave us "blessings" — fruits that grow on the mountain. The holy mountain Sinai is rocky throughout, so that not even a bush grows on it. But down below, near the foot of the mountains, around either the central peak or the peaks around it, there is a little plot of ground where the holy monks diligently plant little trees and orchards, and set up oratories with cells near them, so they can gather fruits that they apparently have cultivated with their own hands from the soil of the mountain itself.

So after we had taken Communion, and the holy men had given us "blessings," and we had come out the door of the church, I started to ask them to show us the different sites. At that, the holy men were immediately kind enough to show us the various places. They showed us the cave where holy Moses was when he had gone up again to the mountain of God to receive the second set of tablets, after he had broken the first when the people sinned. They were also kind enough to show us the other sites we wanted to see, and the ones they knew very well themselves.

But I want you to know, ladies, reverend sisters, that from the place where we were standing, right outside the walls of the church — from the peak of the central mountain, that is — those mountains that we could hardly climb at first seemed so far below us, compared with the one we were standing on, that they looked like little hills. Yet they had been so huge that I thought I had never seen higher mountains, except that this central one far exceeded them. From that spot, we saw Egypt and Palestine, and the Red Sea and the Parthenian Sea [the eastern Mediterranean], which leads to Alexandria and the vast territories of the Saracens. They were all so far below us, we could hardly believe it, but the holy men pointed out each one of them to us.

— *Pilgrimage of Etheria*

Visiting Thecla's Memorial

On her way back to Constantinople (by this time the capital and greatest city of the Roman Empire), Egeria stops at the church dedicated to St. Thecla (famous in Christian story as the companion of Paul) and the memorial to the martyr St. Euphemia.

It would be hard to find a better illustration of the revolution Christianity had made in the lives of women. Here is a woman setting out to tour the memorials of famous Christian heroes (many of them women), staying in communities where women are in positions of authority, and enduring the same ascetic hardships that dedicated men are enduring. The most wildly radical pagan philosopher would hardly have dared to propose such a complete upending of the traditional role of women in society. Yet, for the Christians, it was not just some abstract speculation: it was everyday life.

After I set out from Tarsus, I came to a city by the sea, still in Cilicia, called Pompeiopolis. From there I crossed the border into Hisauria, and on the third day I came to a city in Hisauria called Seleucia.

As soon as I arrived, I went to the bishop, a truly holy man who used to be a monk, and in that city I saw a very beautiful church. But since it was about fifteen hundred paces from there to St. Thecla, which is on a low hill outside the city, I decided to go there instead to make the stay I intended.

There is nothing at the holy church in that place except innumerable cells of men and women. I found a very dear friend of mine there. All of the East bears witness to the way she lives. She is a holy deaconess named Marthana. I had known her at Jerusalem, where she had gone to pray. Here she was ruling over the cells of the apotactites[16] and virgins. I just can't describe how happy she was to see me, and I to see her.

But back to what we were talking about: There are very many cells on the hill, and in the middle of the hill is a great wall enclosing the church, which contains the beautiful memorial. The wall was built to guard the church from the Hisauri, who are very ill natured and often commit robbery, to keep them from trying to rob the monastery established there.

When I got there, in the name of God, we prayed at the memorial. The whole *Acts of St. Thecla* was read, and then I gave thanks to Christ our God, who was pleased to fulfill my desires in everything, though I am unworthy and undeserving.

I stayed there two days, seeing the holy monks and apotactites who were there, both men and women. I prayed and took Communion there. Then I went back to Tarsus and resumed my journey.

I stayed three days at Tarsus; then I set out on my journey, in the name of God. I arrived at a station called Mansocrenae the same day and stayed there. The next day I went past Mount Tarsus; then I took a route I was already familiar with, through all the provinces I had crossed on my way out: Cappadocia, Galatia, and Bithynia. I arrived at Chalcedon, where I stayed to see the very well-known memorial of the martyrdom of St. Euphemia, which I was already familiar with from before.

The next day I crossed the sea and arrived at Constantinople. I gave thanks to Christ our God, who was pleased to give me such grace, though I am undeserving and unworthy: he gave me not only the will to go but also the ability to walk through the places I wanted to see, and at last to come back to Constantinople.

When I got there, I went through all the Churches of the Apostles, and all the memorials to martyrs, of which there are very many. And I never stopped giving thanks to Christ our God, who was thus pleased to grant me his mercy.

So from here I send you these letters, dear ladies, light of my eyes. And I have already decided, in the name of Christ our God, to go to Ephesus in Asia to pray, because that is where the memorial of the holy and blessed apostle John is. And if I am still in the body after that, and I am able to see any other places, I will either (if God permits me to do it) tell you about them in person, dear ladies, or — if I have some other project in mind —I will tell you about it in a letter.

But you, dear ladies, light of my eyes, be good enough to remember me, whether I am in the body or out of the body.

PILGRIMAGE OF ETHERIA

Mothers of the Church

Notes

1. Celsus, quoted in Origen, *Against Celsus,* 2.55.
2. Rodney Stark, *The Rise of Christianity* (San Francisco: HarperCollins, 1997), 111f.
3. *Passion of Perpetua and Felicity,* 3.
4. "*Tu nos, inquiunt, te autem Deus,*" which means, literally: " 'You, us,' they said, 'but God, you.' " This was an idea easily conveyed by pointing and nodding, so that the whole audience would understand.
5. Roman citizens had certain legal immunities to cruel punishments; see, for example, Acts 22:23-29.
6. St. Ambrose, *On Virginity,* 1.2.
7. "Quirites" is an ancient name for citizens of the city of Rome.
8. By this time, Gregory was bishop of Nyssa, now in modern Turkey.
9. J. N. D. Kelly, *Jerome: His Life, Writings, and Controversies* (New York: Harper & Row, 1975), p. 95, quoting Jerome's letters 28, 29, and 34.
10. St. Jerome, Letter 127.
11. St. Augustine, *Confessions,* 5.8.
12. St. Augustine, *Confessions,* 9.10-11.
13. This is another name for Constantinople as the capital of the Roman Empire.
14. Socrates Scholasticus, *Church History,* 1.17.
15. St. Augustine, Letter 130.
16. These were women who had renounced all their possessions.

About the Authors

MIKE AQUILINA is author or editor of more than thirty books, including *The Fathers of the Church* and *The Mass of the Early Christians*. His works have been translated into many languages, from Hungarian and Portuguese to German and braille. Mike has co-hosted eight series that air on the Eternal Word Television Network. He is solo host of two feature-length documentaries on the early Christians.

CHRISTOPHER BAILEY has written about Christian history in books, magazines, and the *New Catholic Encyclopedia*. He is co-author of *Praying the Psalms with the Early Christians* and *The Doubter's Novena* and author of *Dr. Boli's Encyclopedia of Misinformation*. He has been named one of the funniest Christian writers in America by the Associated Church Press.